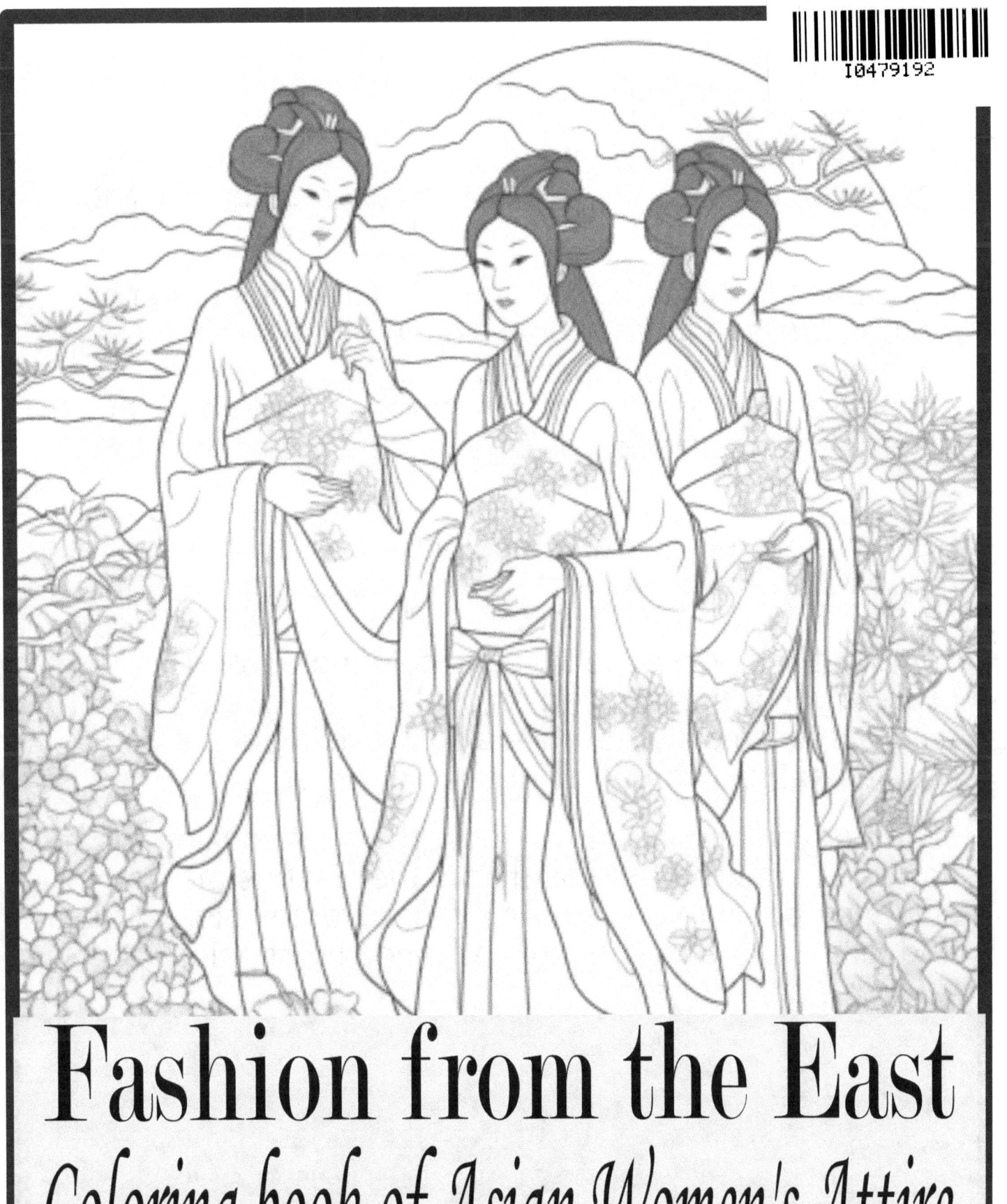

Fashion from the East
Coloring book of Asian Women's Attire

Introduction

Welcome to "Fashion from the East," a coloring book featuring the beautiful and diverse traditional attire of Asian women. This book is a celebration of the vibrant cultures and rich histories that make up Asia.

Each page in this book features a unique illustration of a woman dressed in traditional clothing from various Asian countries. You'll find Japanese kimonos, Chinese cheongsams, Korean hanboks, and many more. With 54 different themes/titles, you'll have plenty of options to choose from.

Coloring is a relaxing and meditative activity that can help reduce stress and anxiety. It's also a creative outlet that allows you to express yourself and explore different color combinations. We hope that this coloring book will provide you with a fun and enjoyable way to learn about different Asian cultures while also providing a relaxing activity that you can enjoy at your leisure.

Whether you're a fan of fashion, art, or just looking for a fun way to unwind, "Fashion from the East" is the perfect coloring book for you. So grab your favorite coloring tools, and let's explore the beauty and diversity of Asian women's attire together

This book belong to

_____

_____

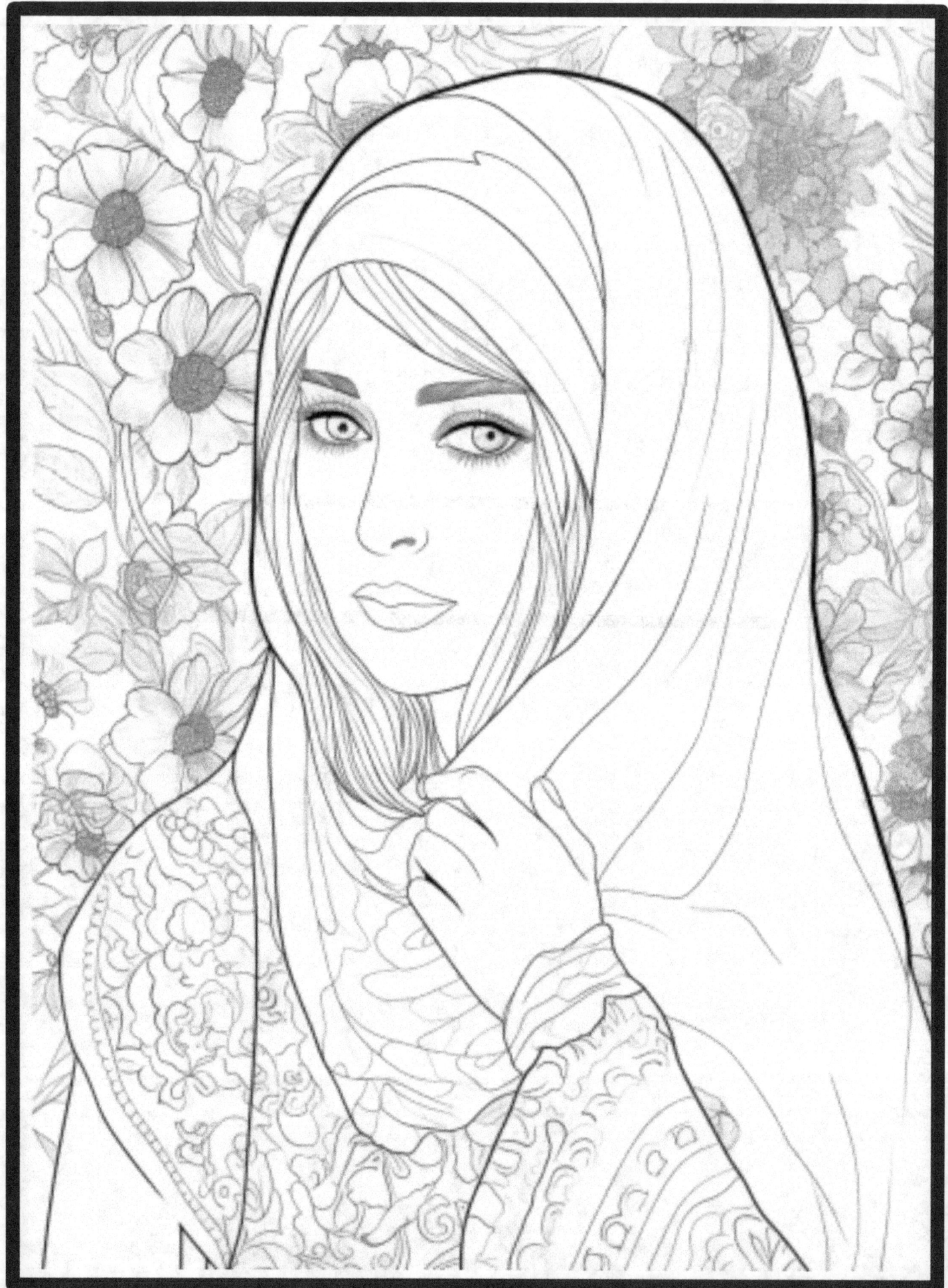

Afgan
Burqa

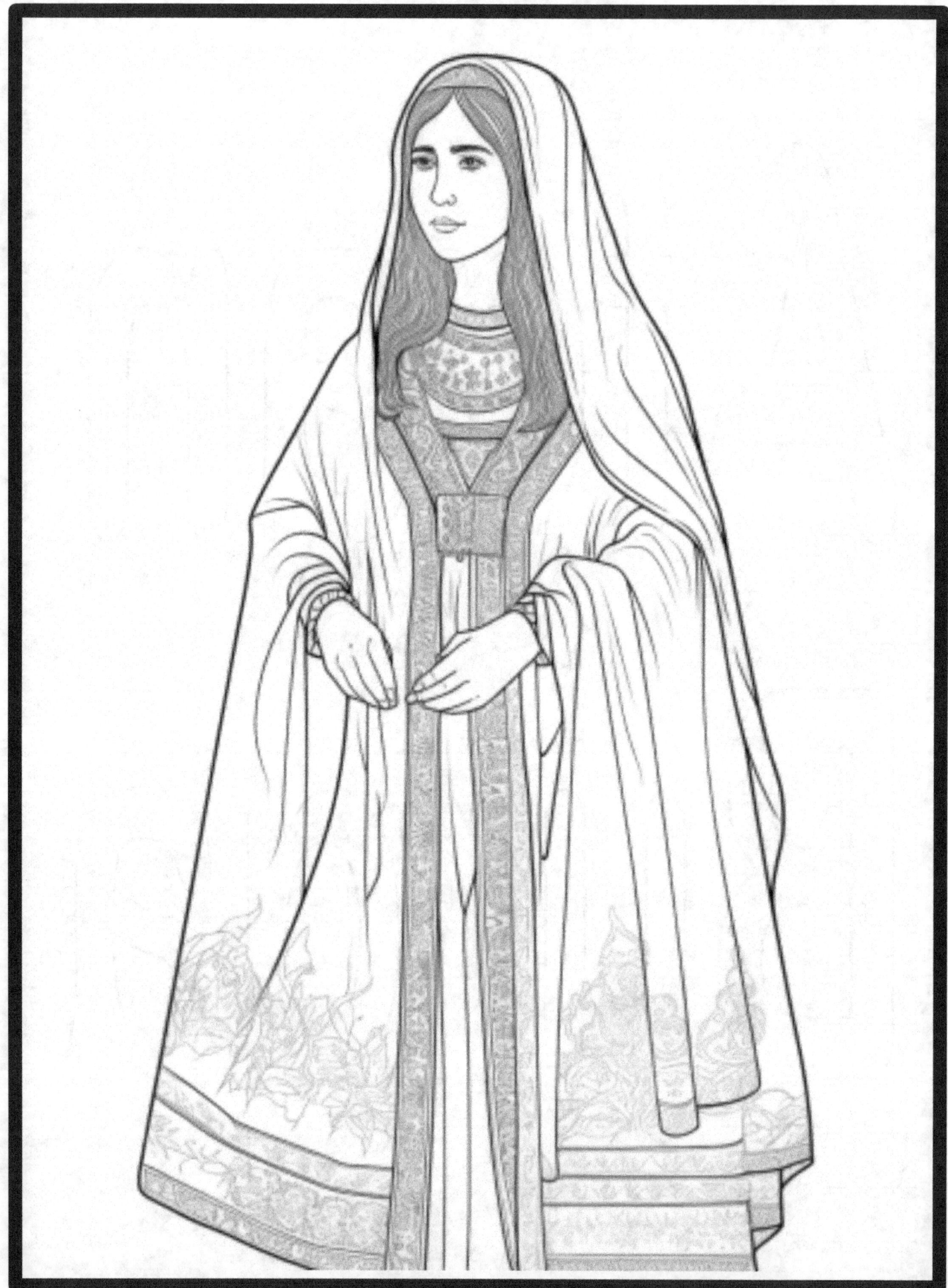

Armenian

Traditional Dress

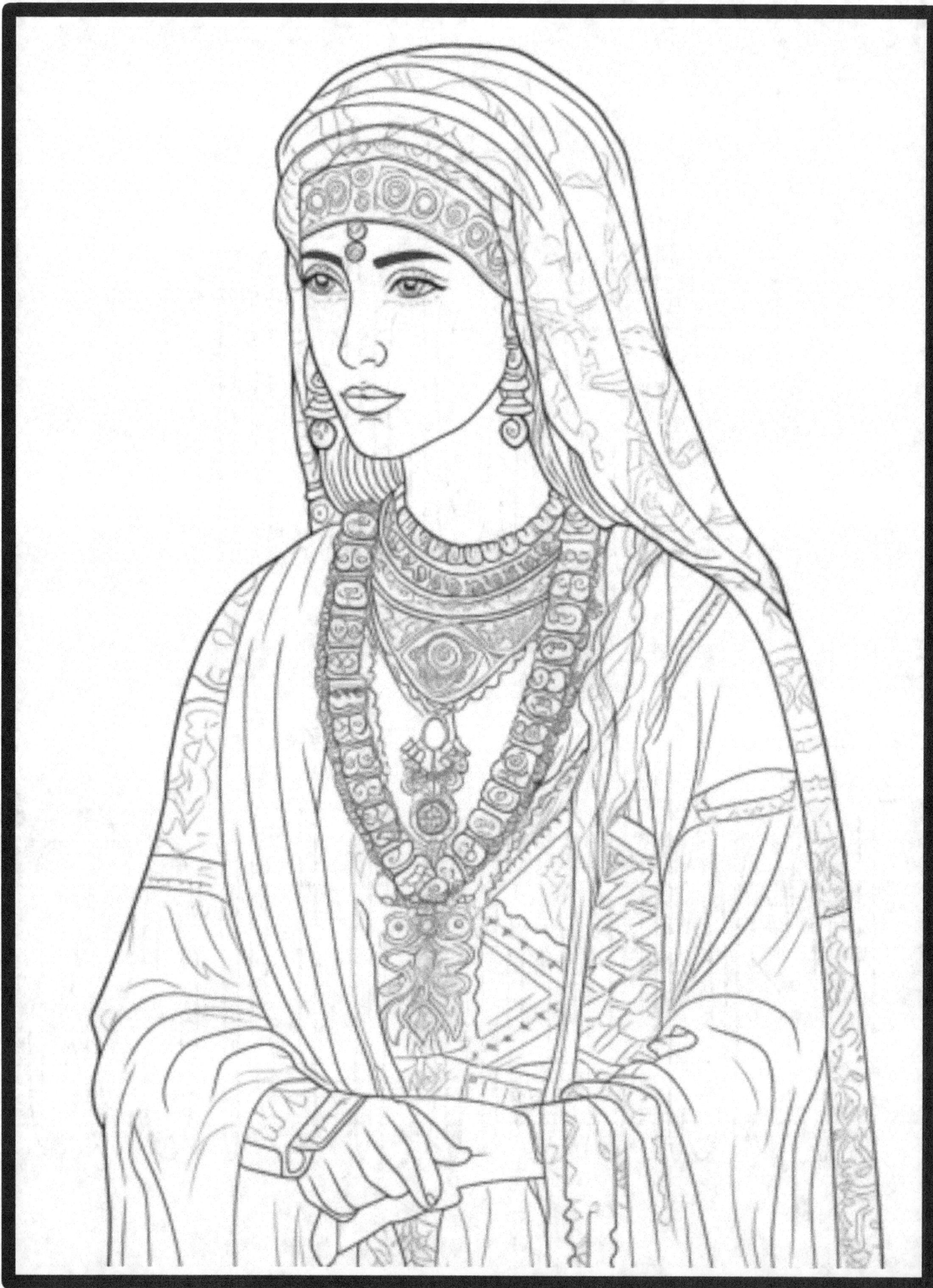

Azebaijani National Dress

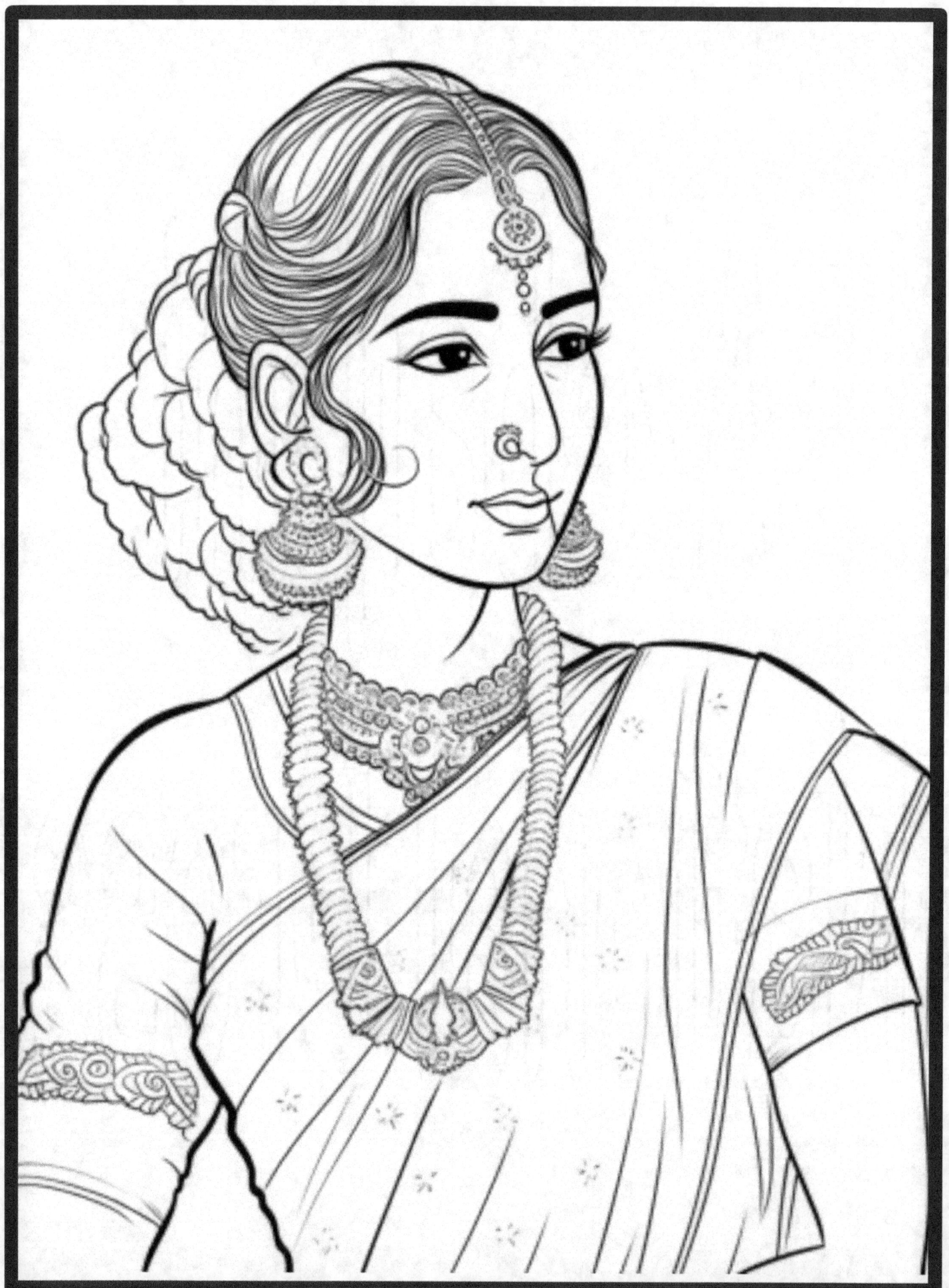

Bengali
Sari

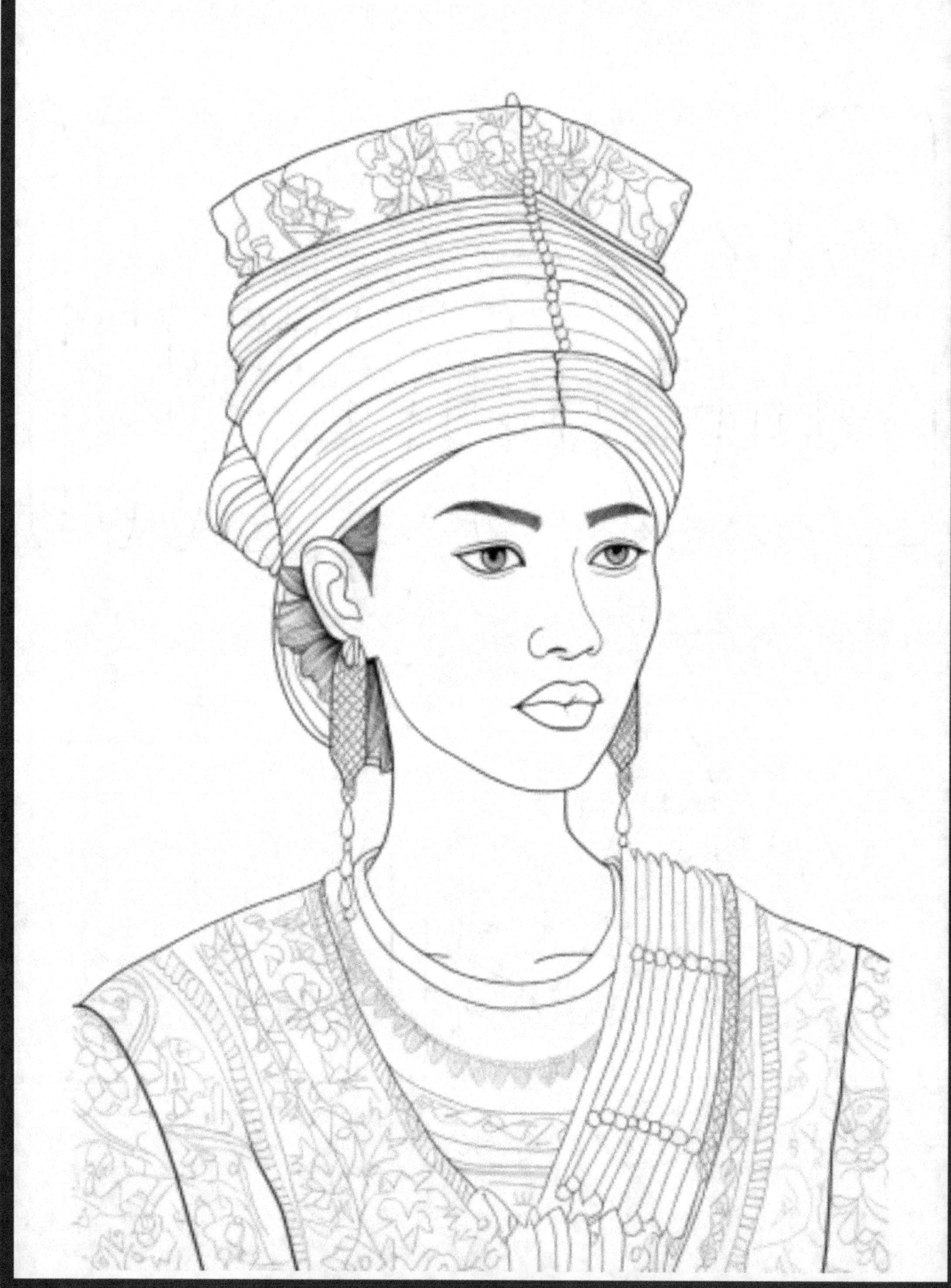

Burmese Longyi

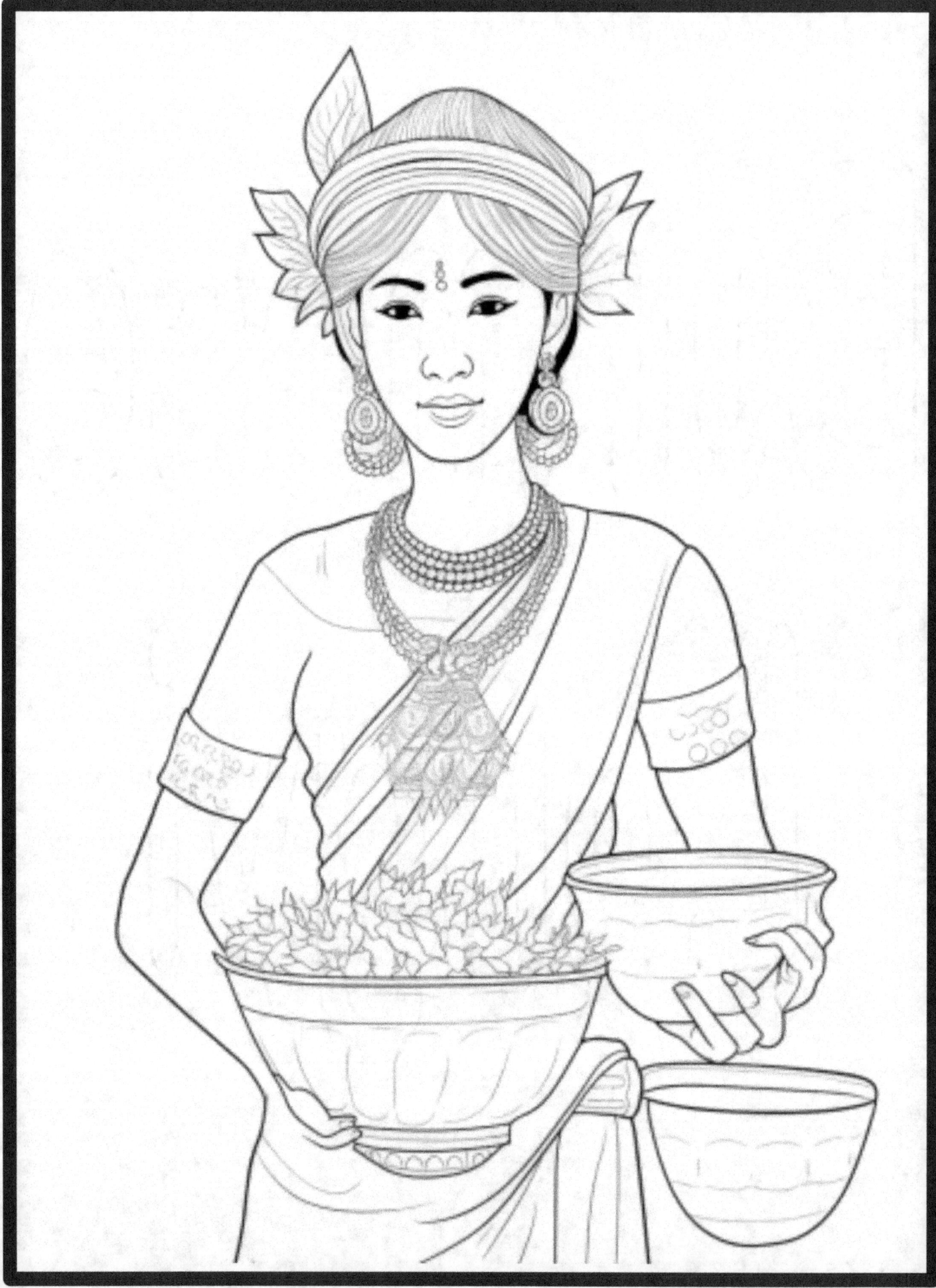

Cambodian

Sampot

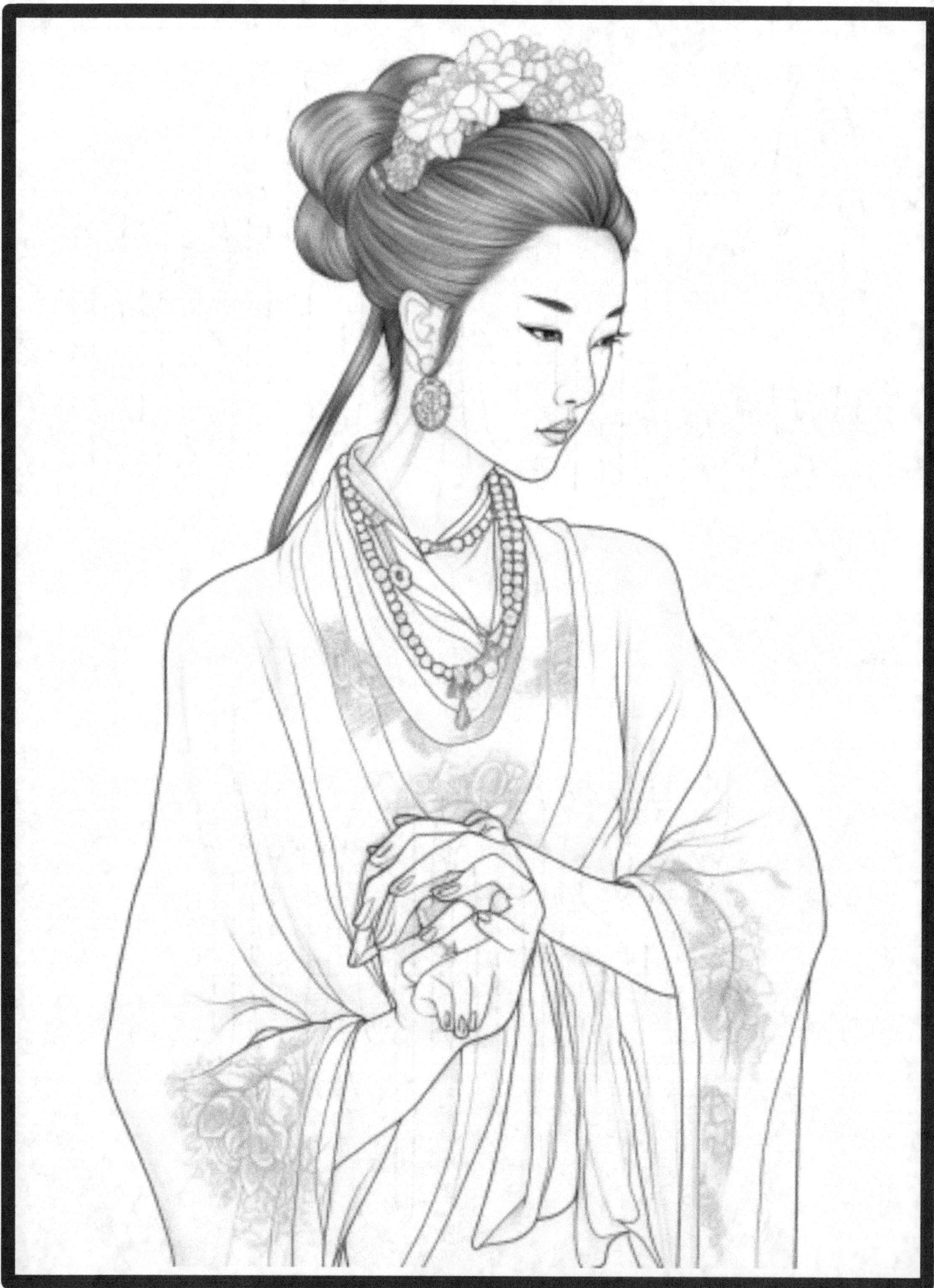

Chinese Qipao

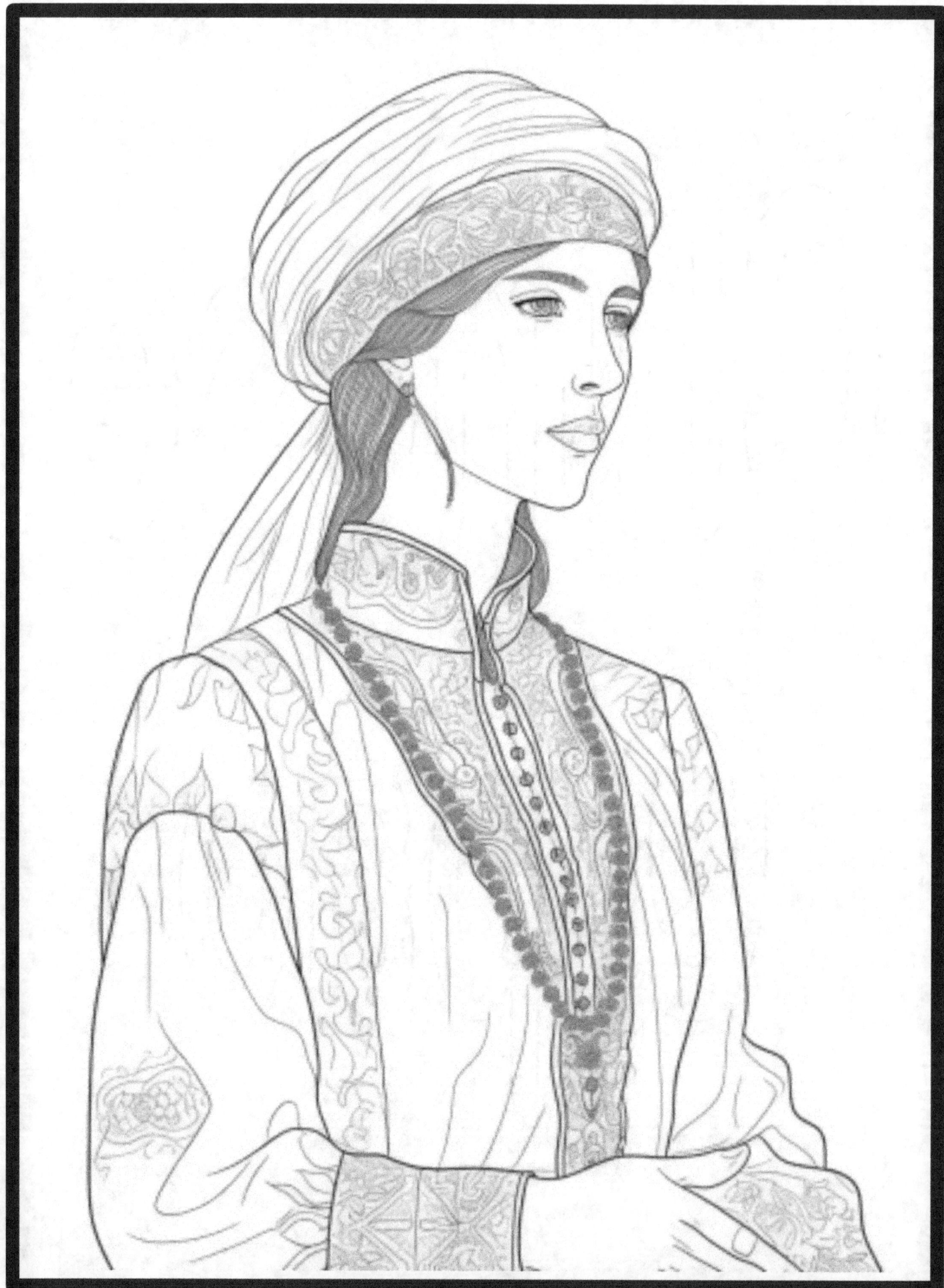

Georgian Chokha

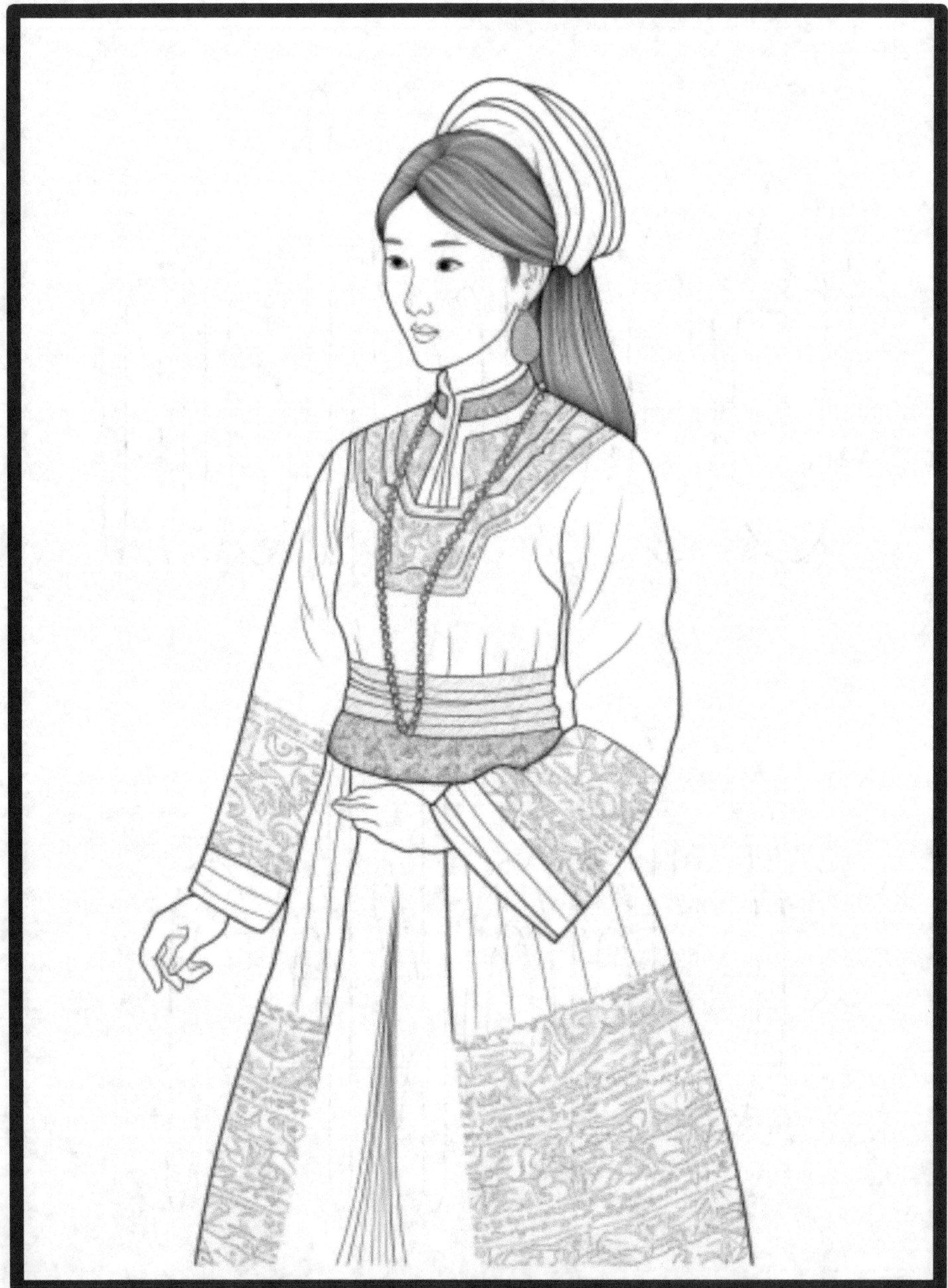

Hmong

Traditional Dress

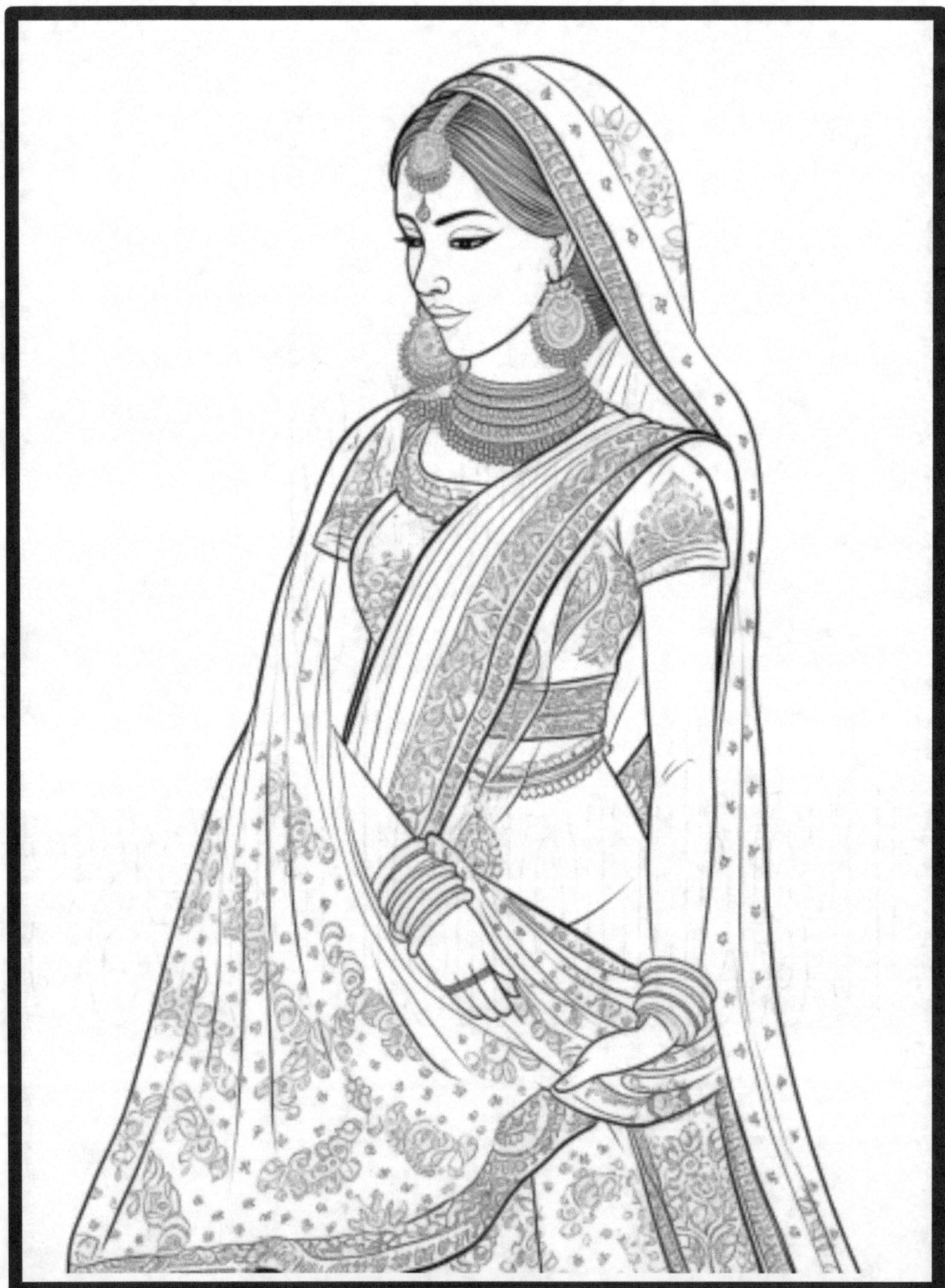

Indian lehenga

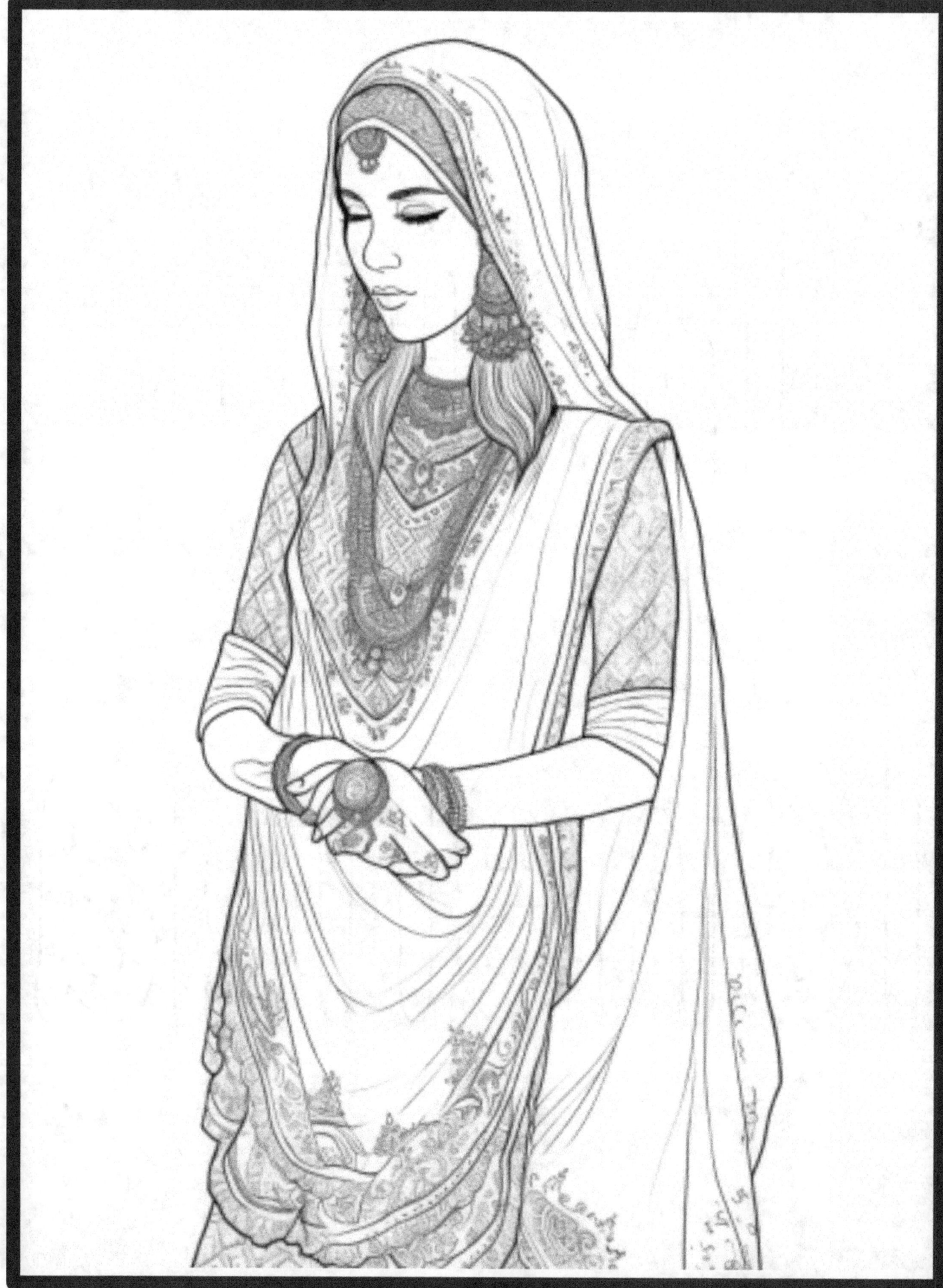

Indian Patiala Salwar

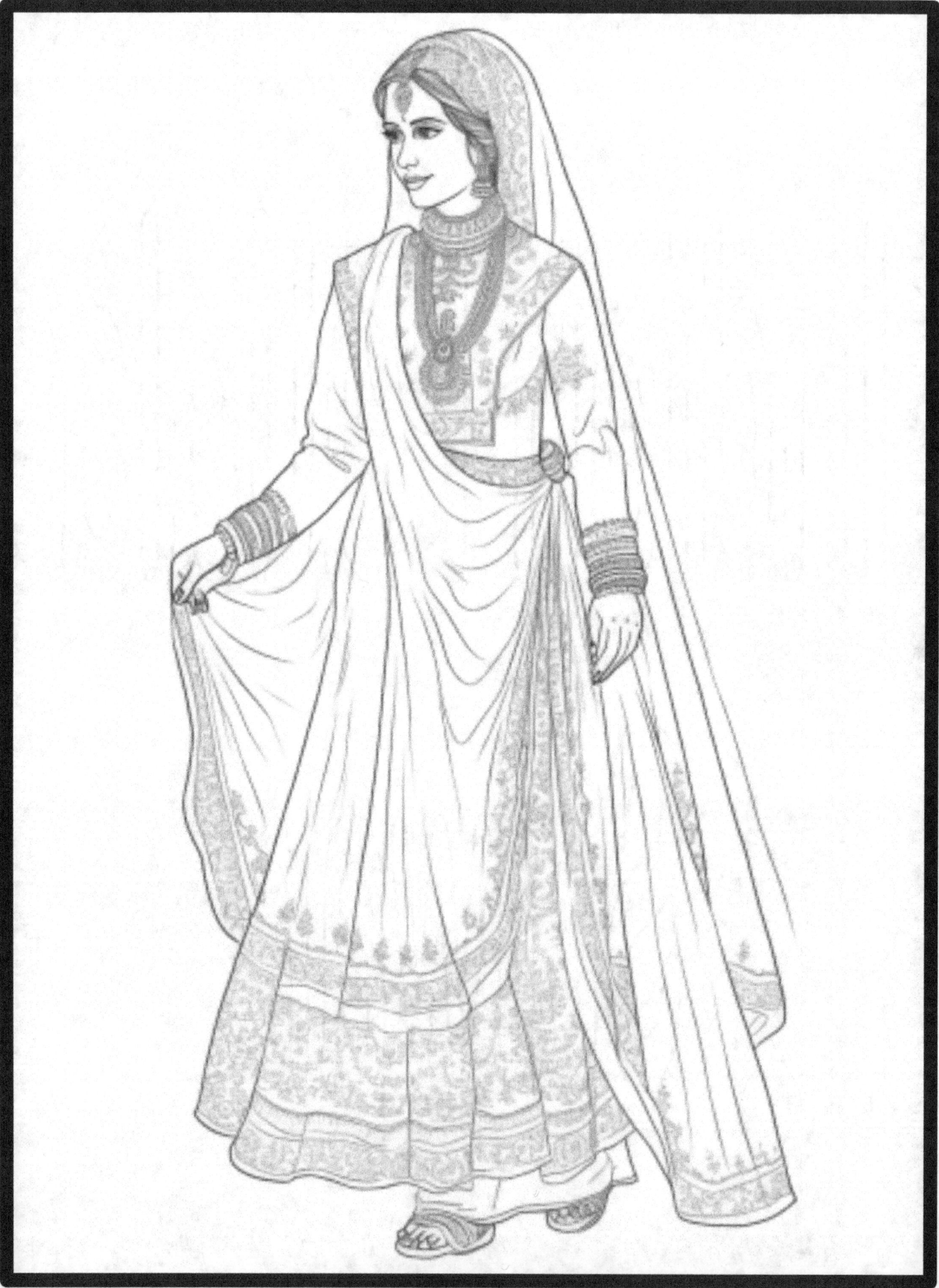

Indian Salwar Kameez

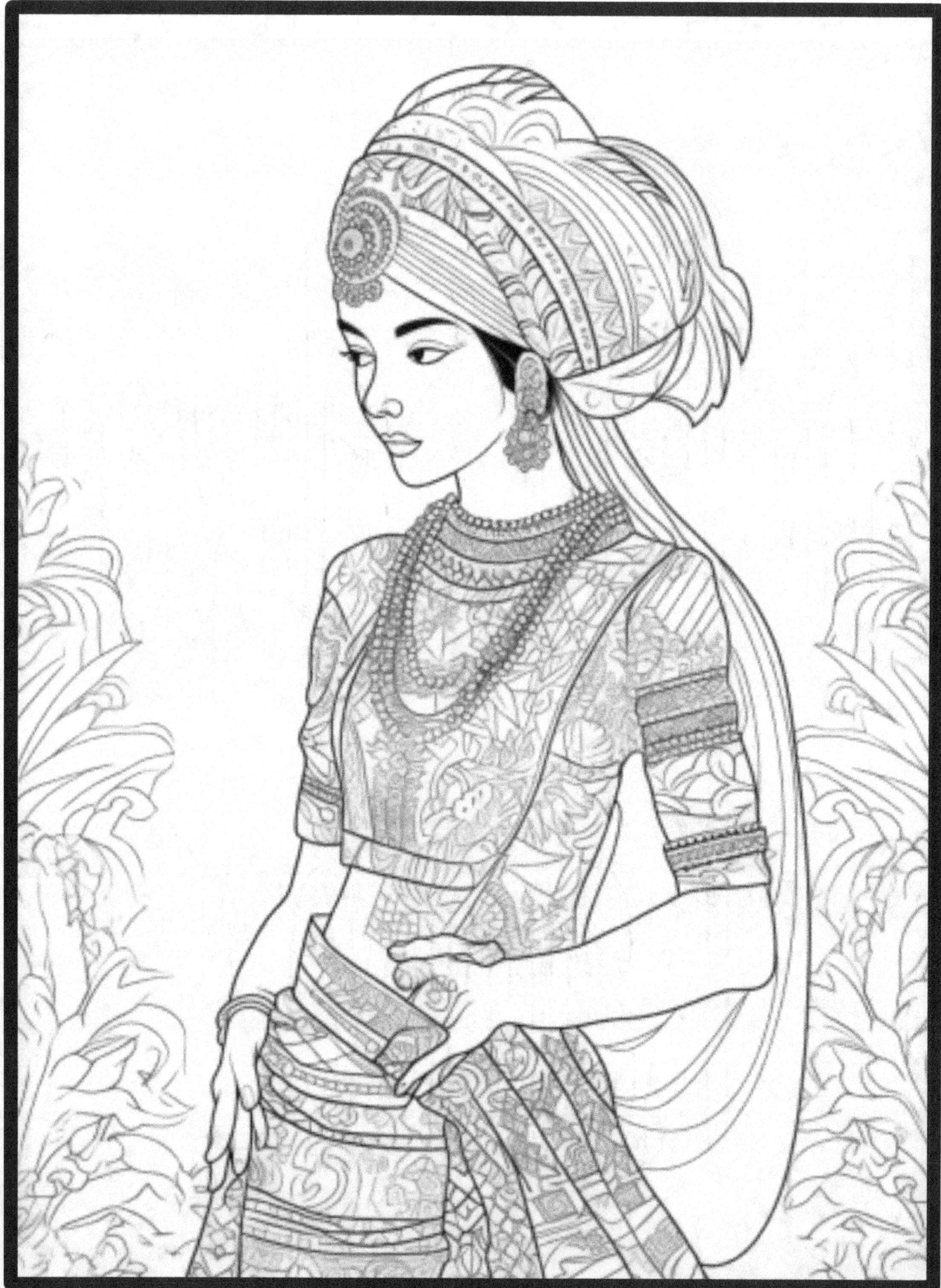

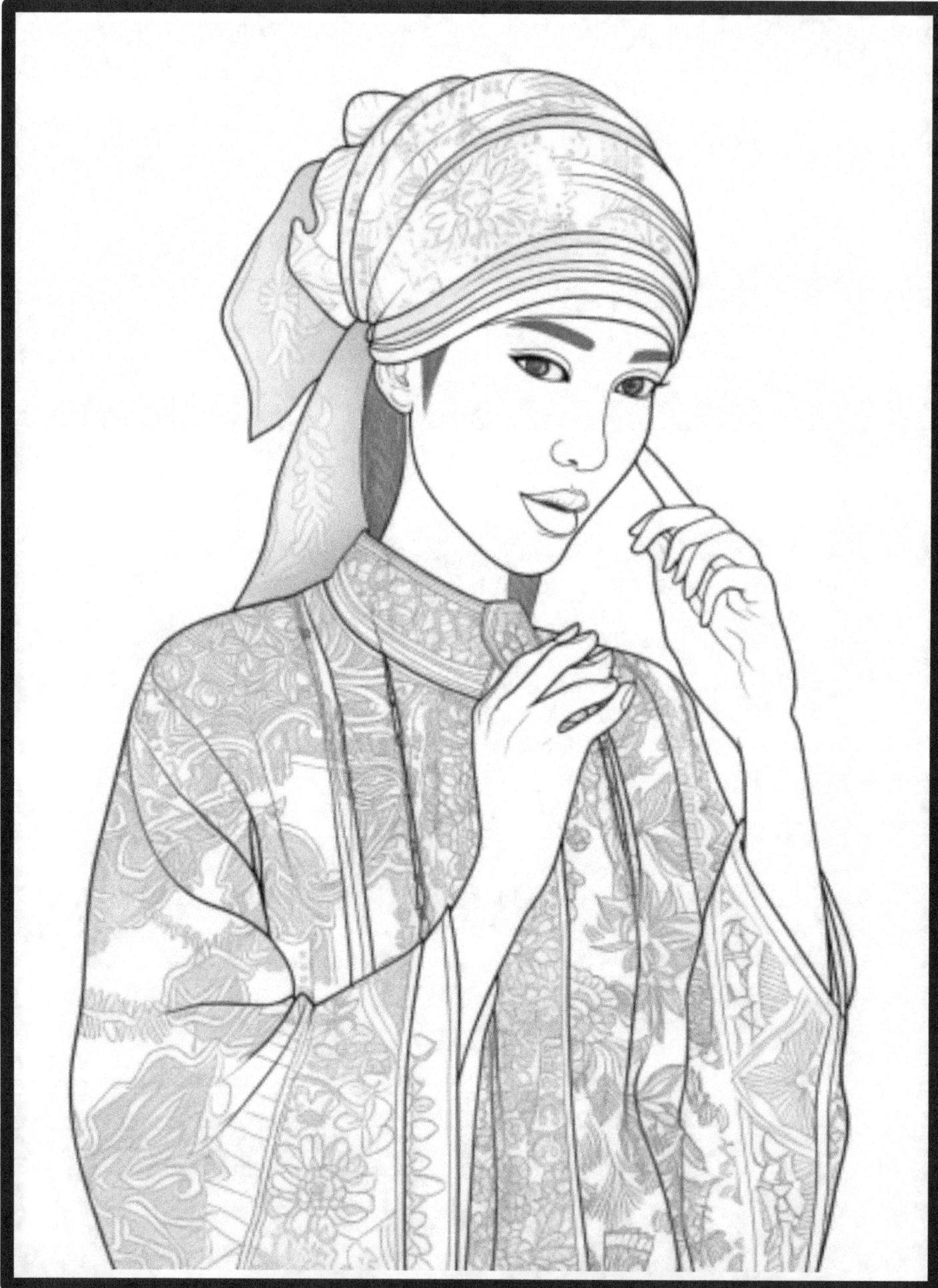

Indonesian

Kain Panjang

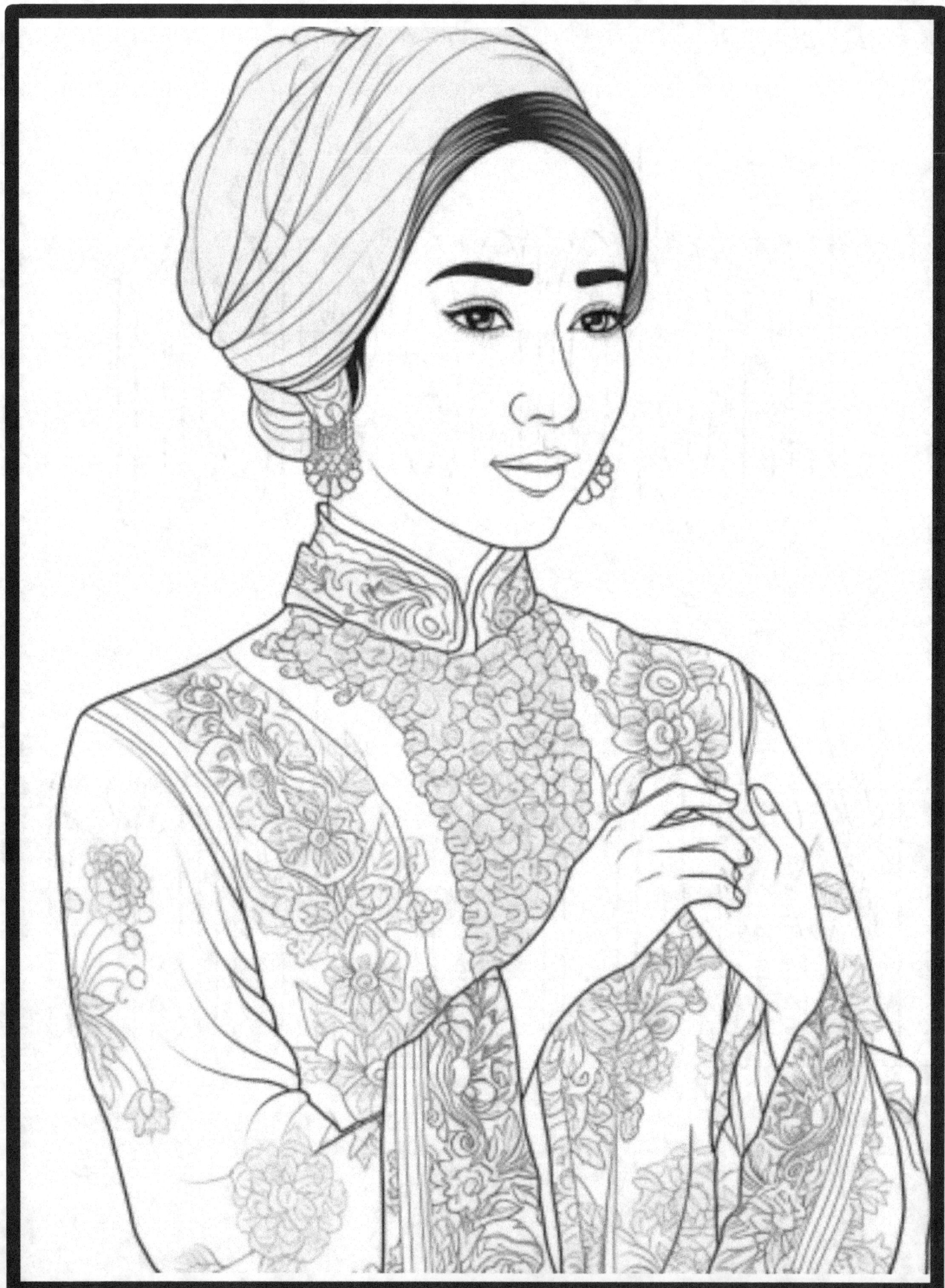

Indonesian

Kebaya

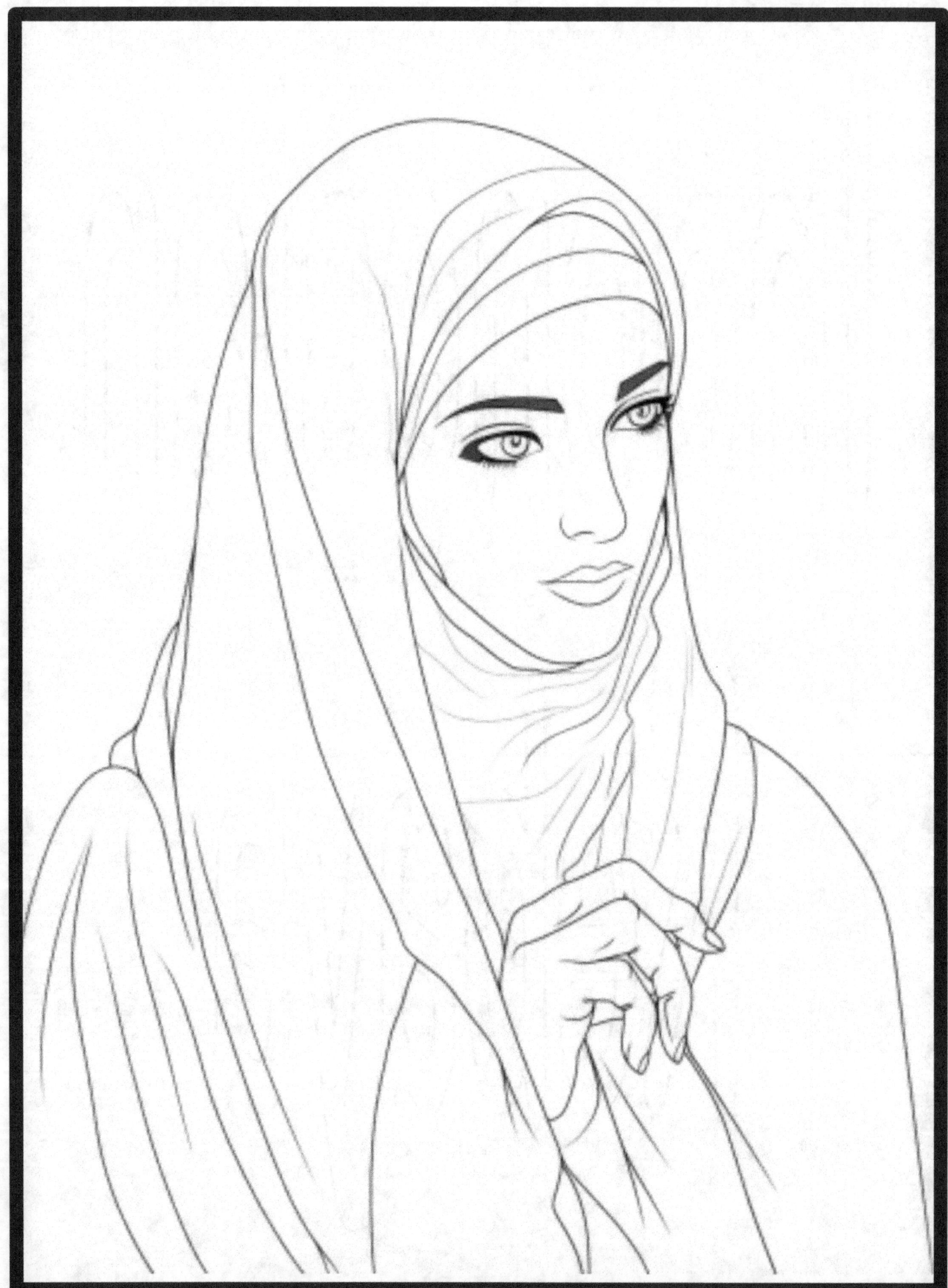

Iranian Chador

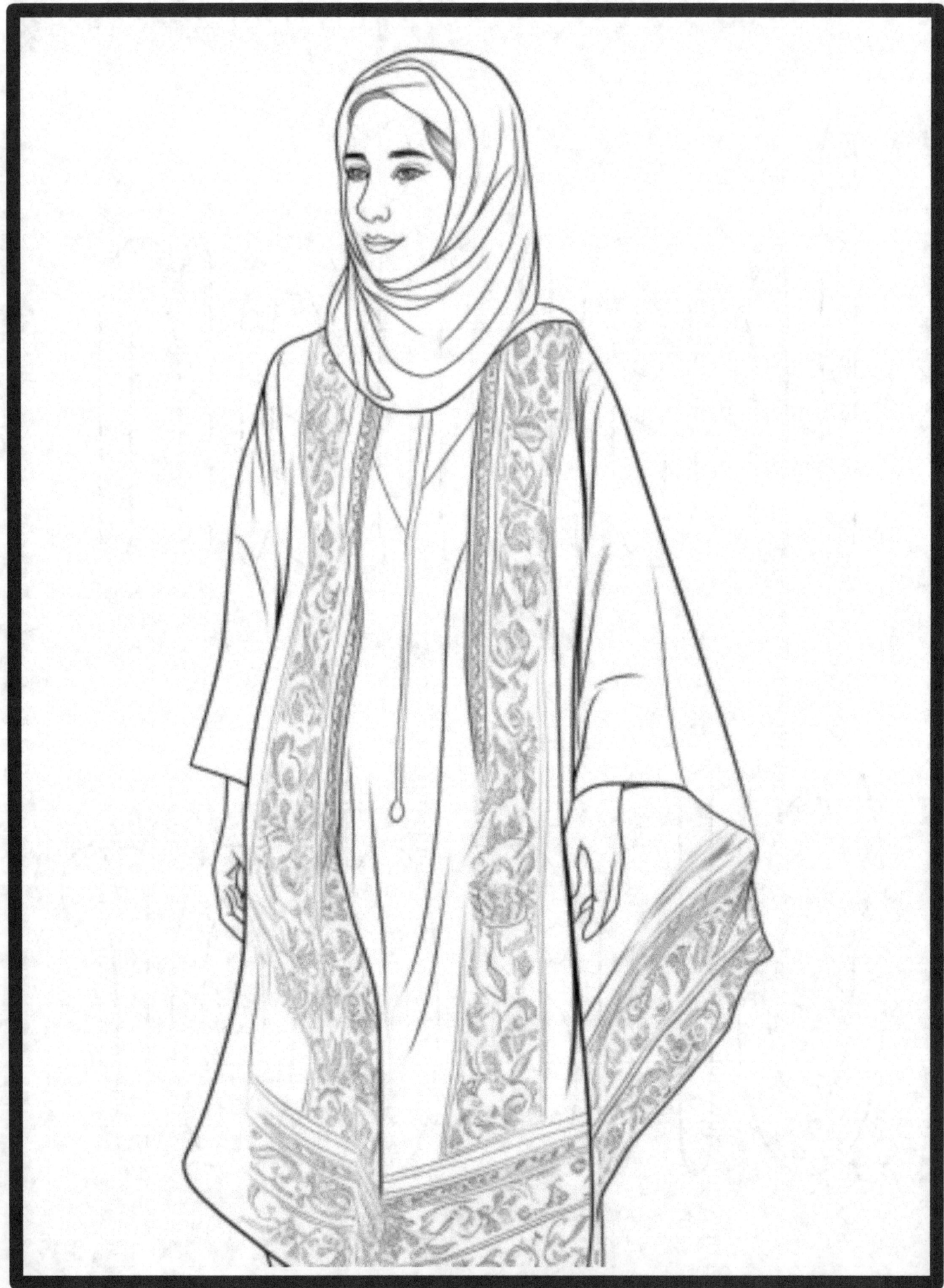

Iranian
Shirtdress

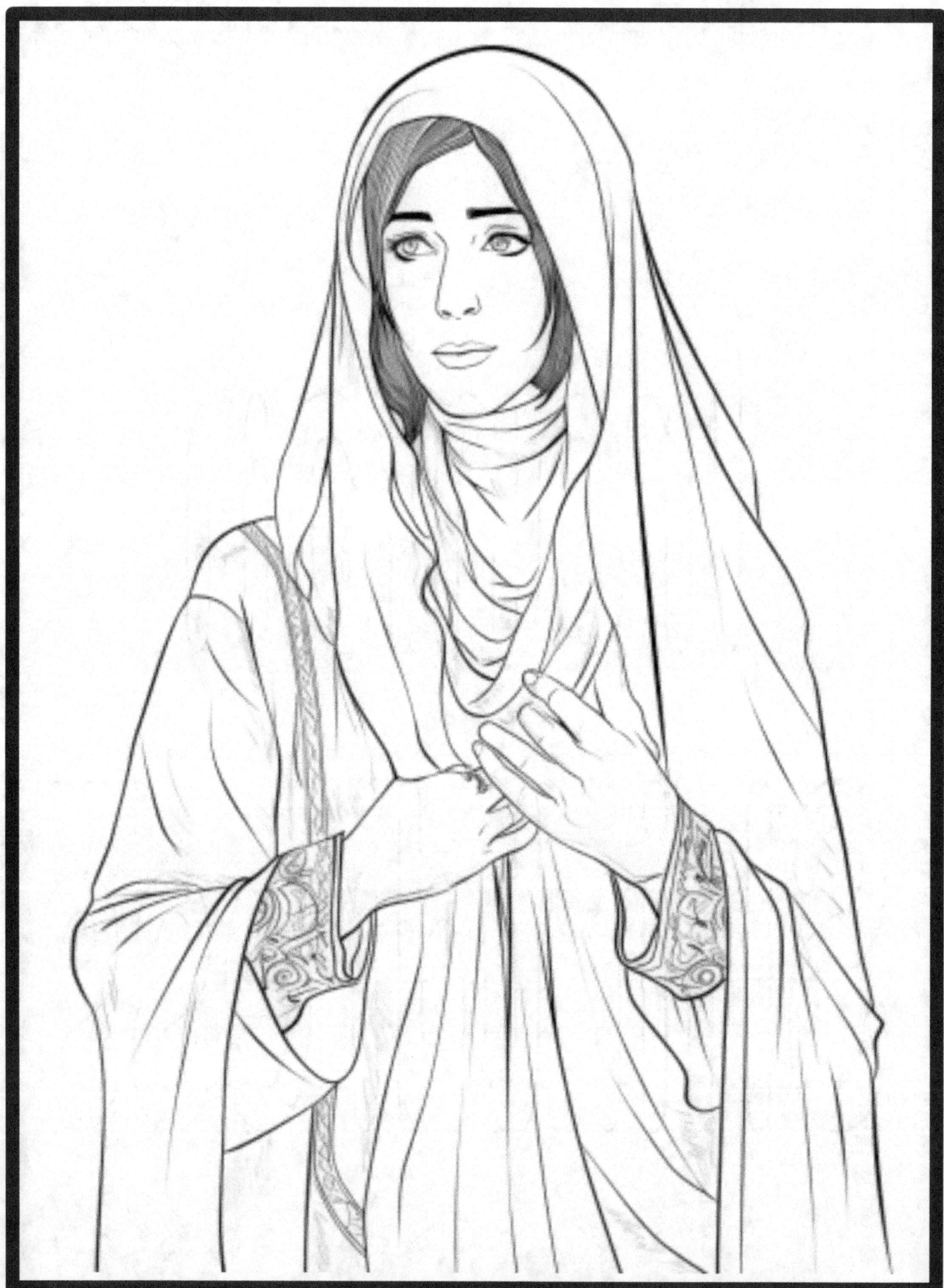

Iraqi

Abaya

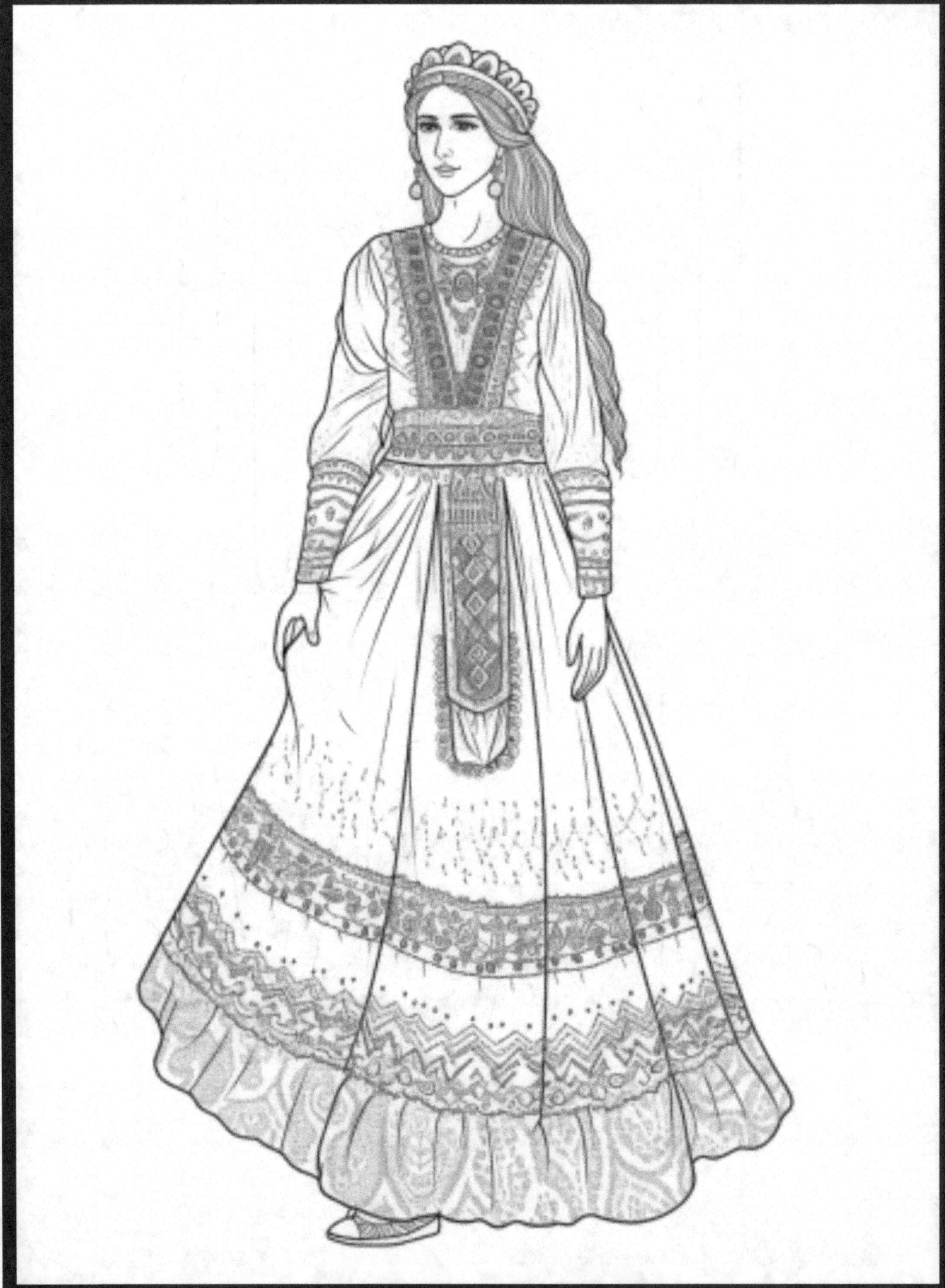

Israel

National Dress

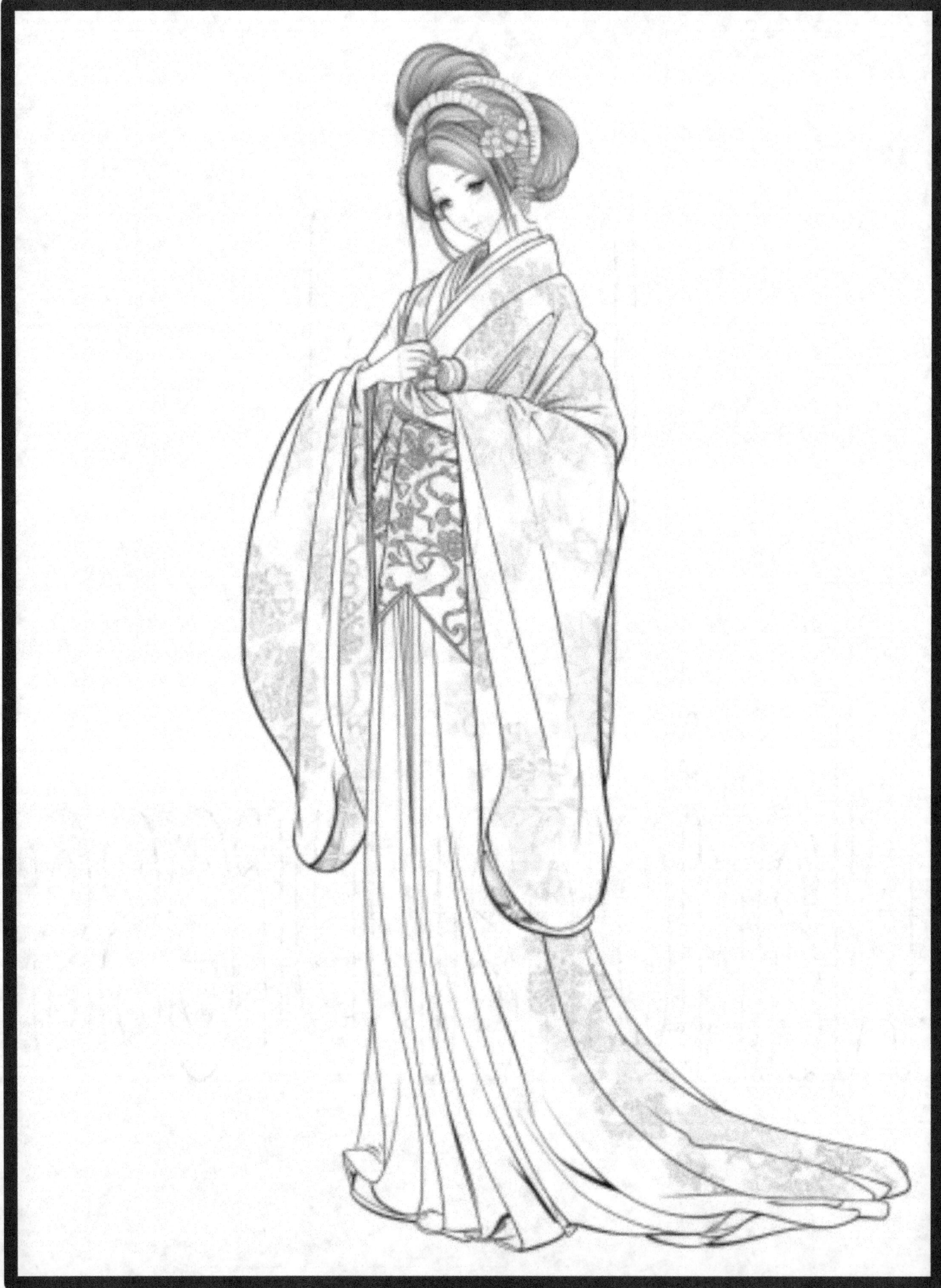

Japanese

Furisode

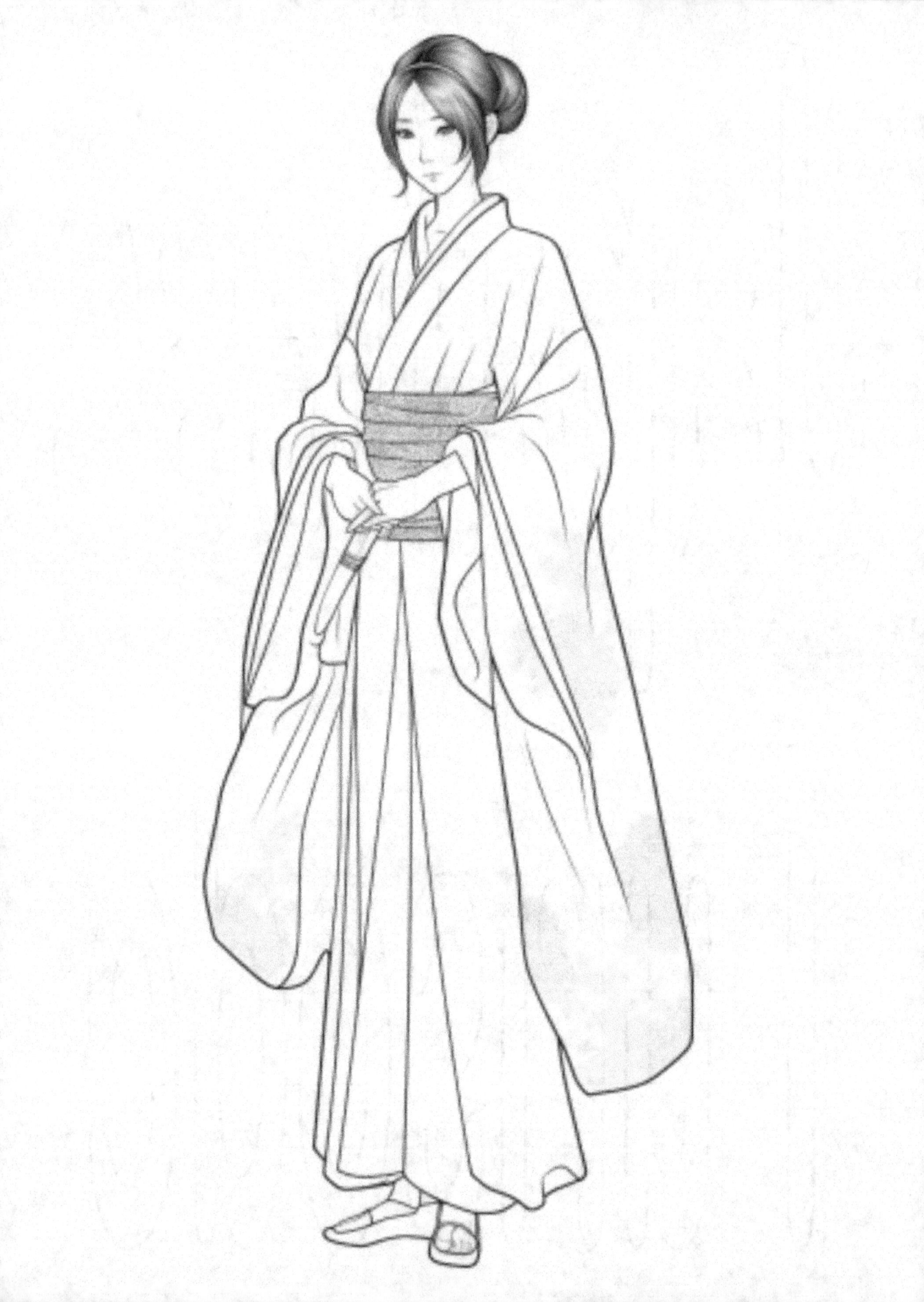

Japanese

Hakaa

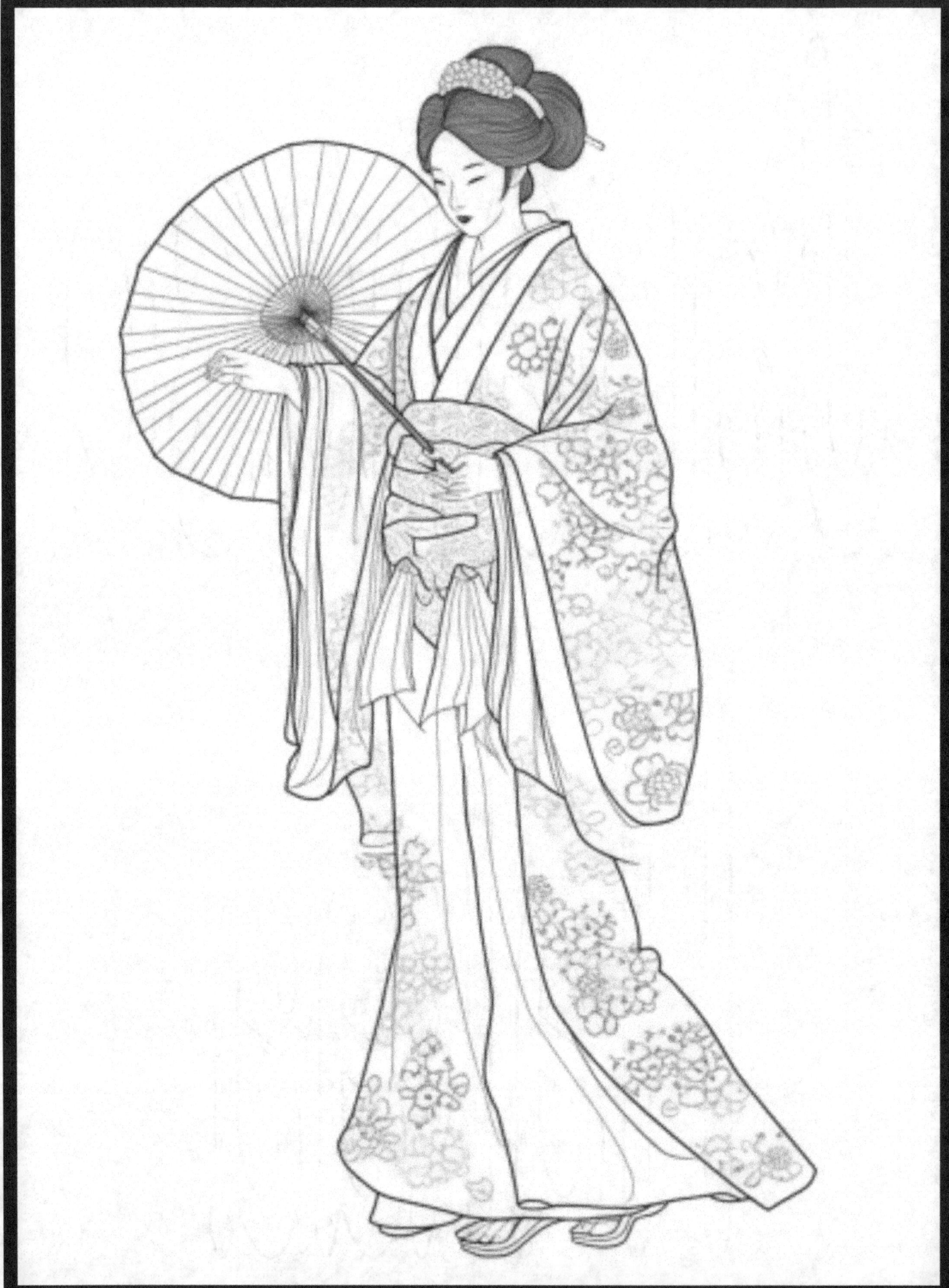

Japanese Hapi

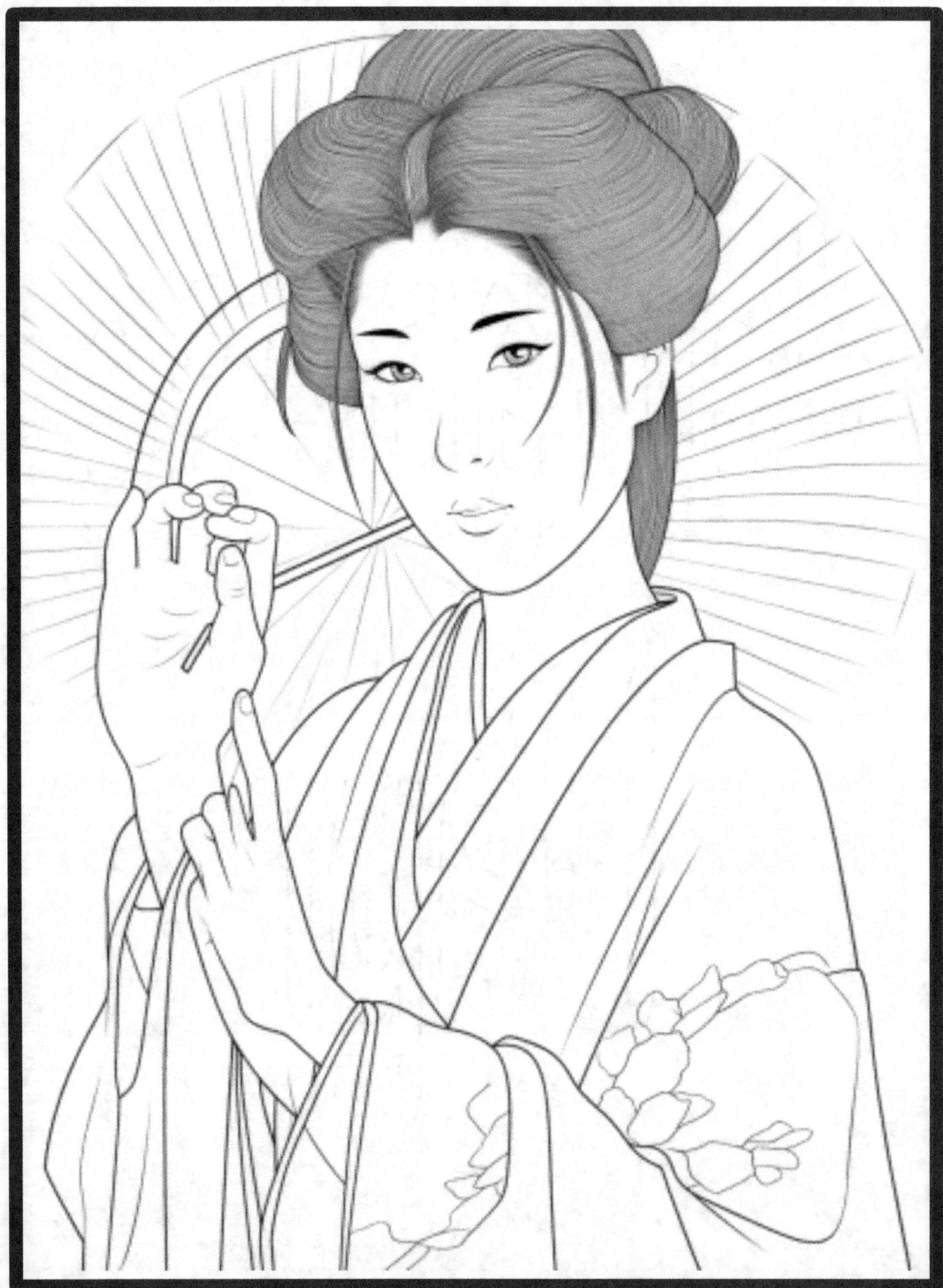

Japanese Jinbei

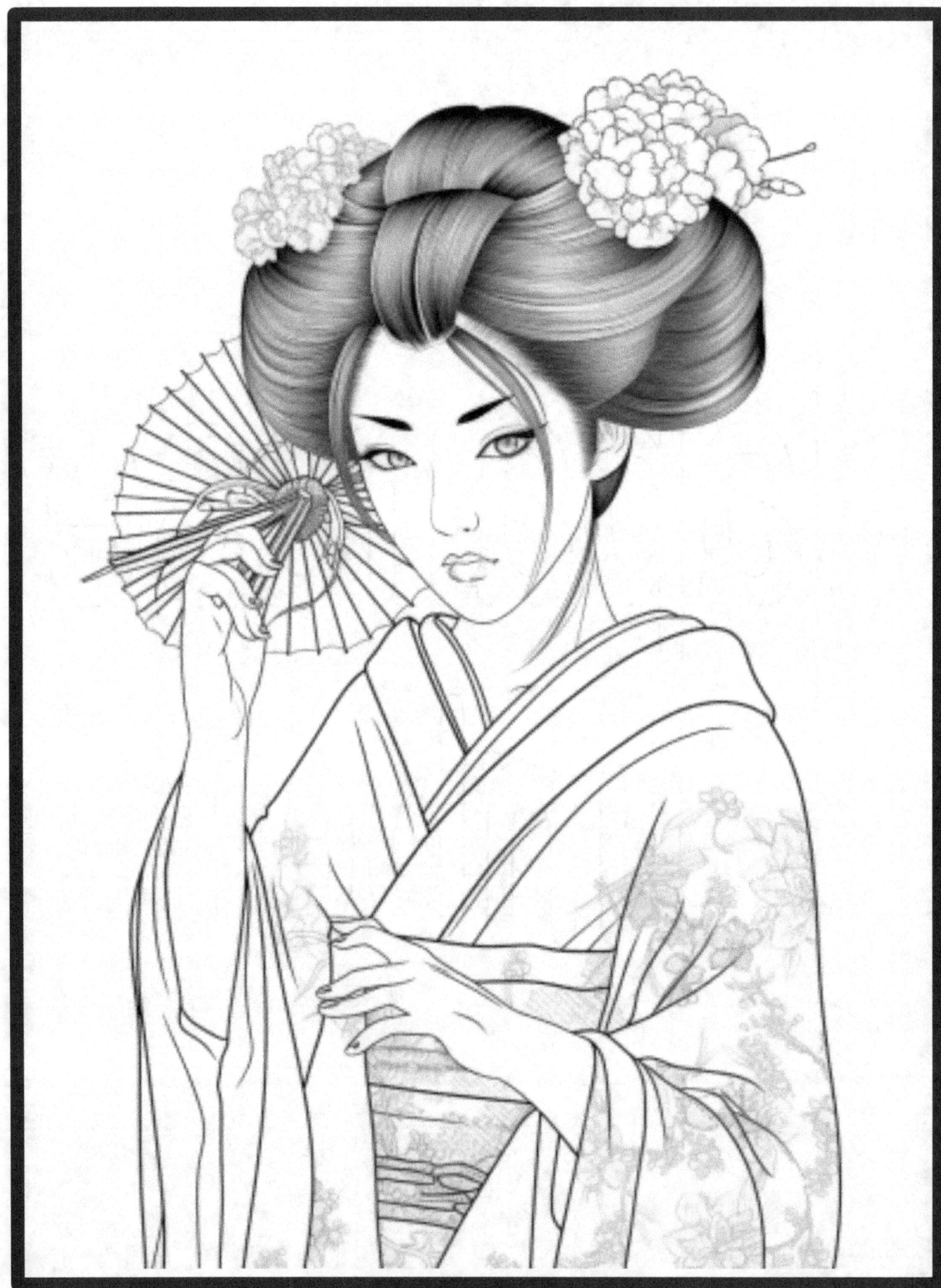

Japanese Kimono

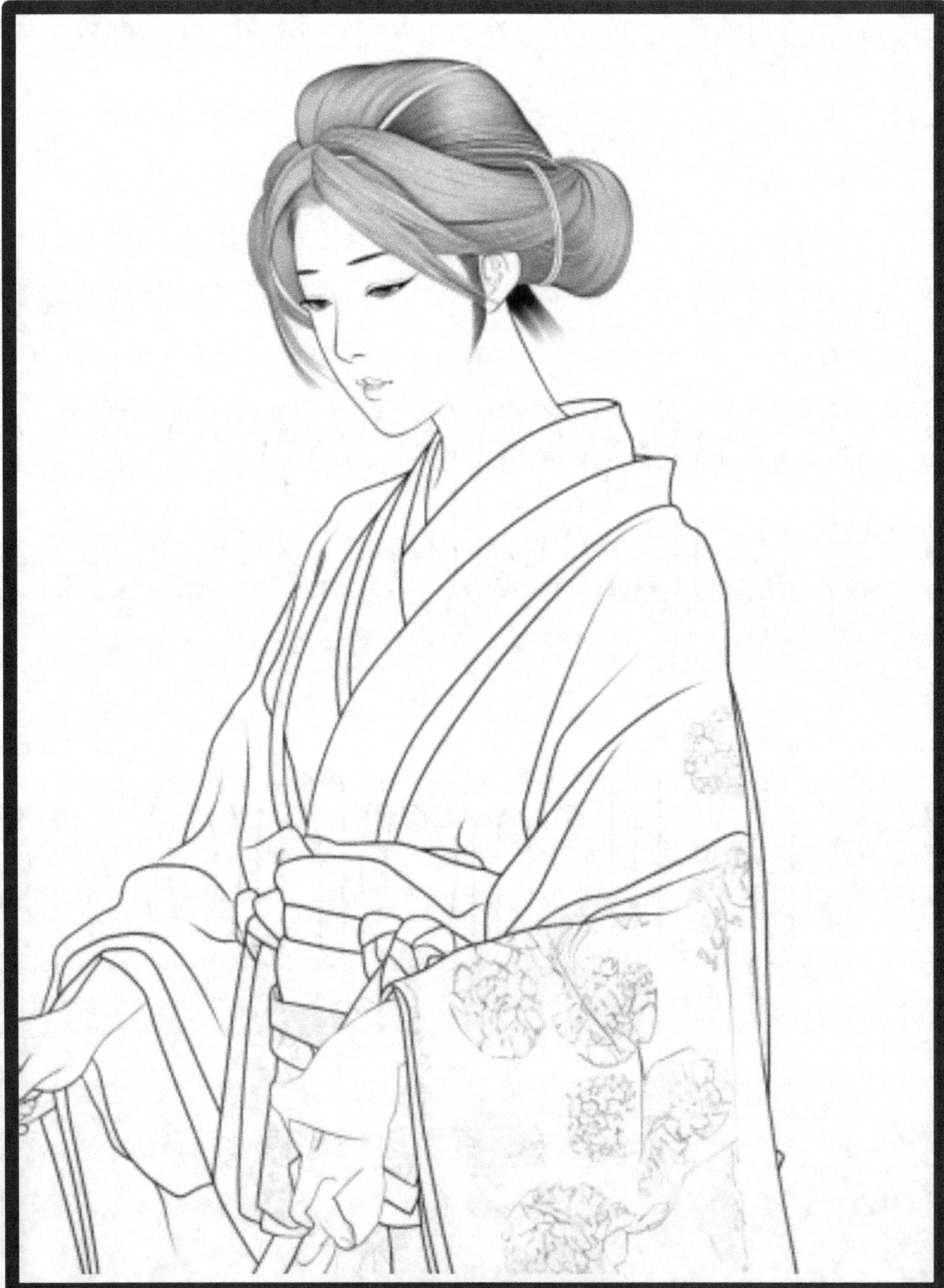

Japanese Yukata

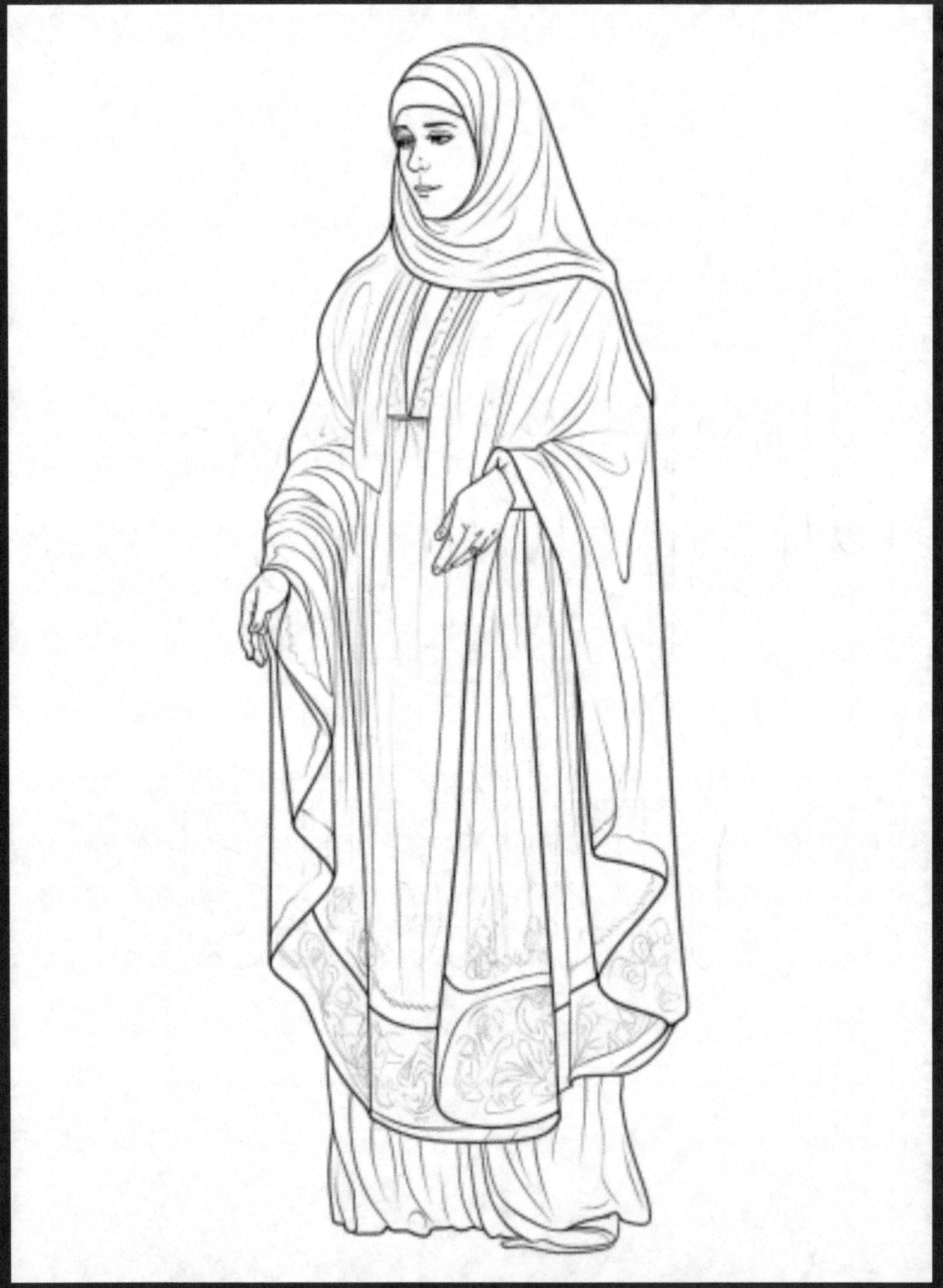

Jordanian

Thobe

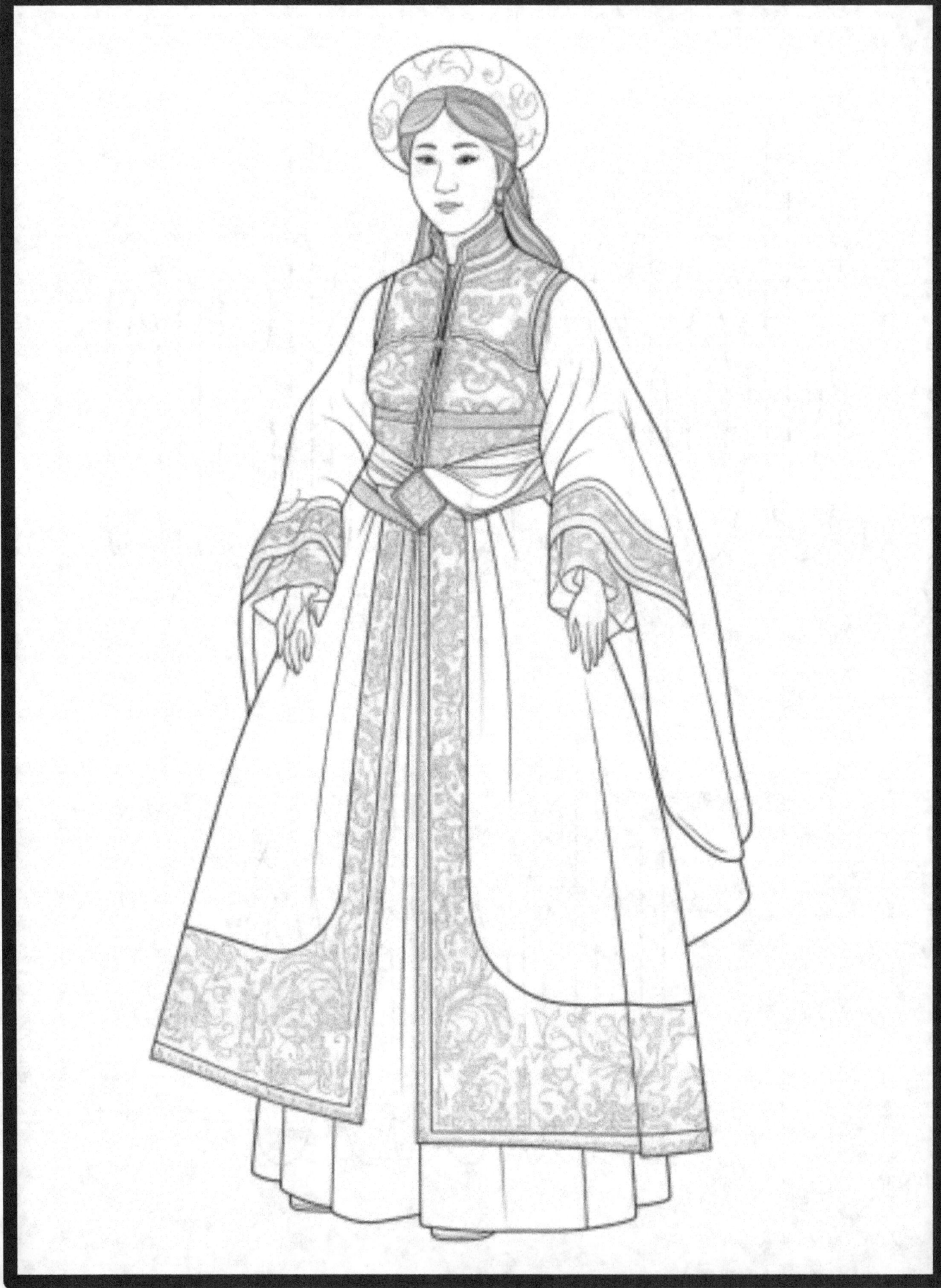

Kazakh

National Dress

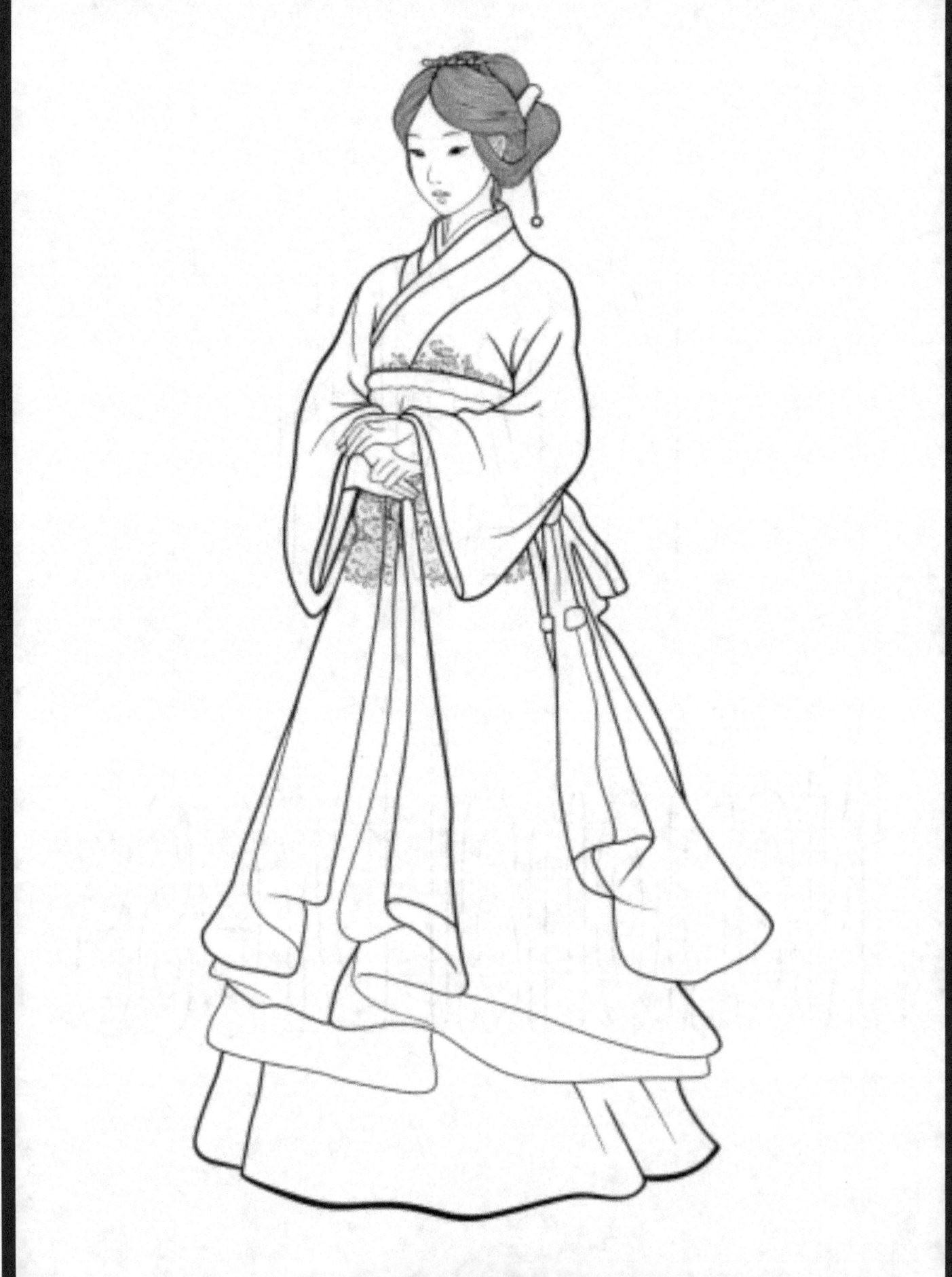

Korean Hanbok

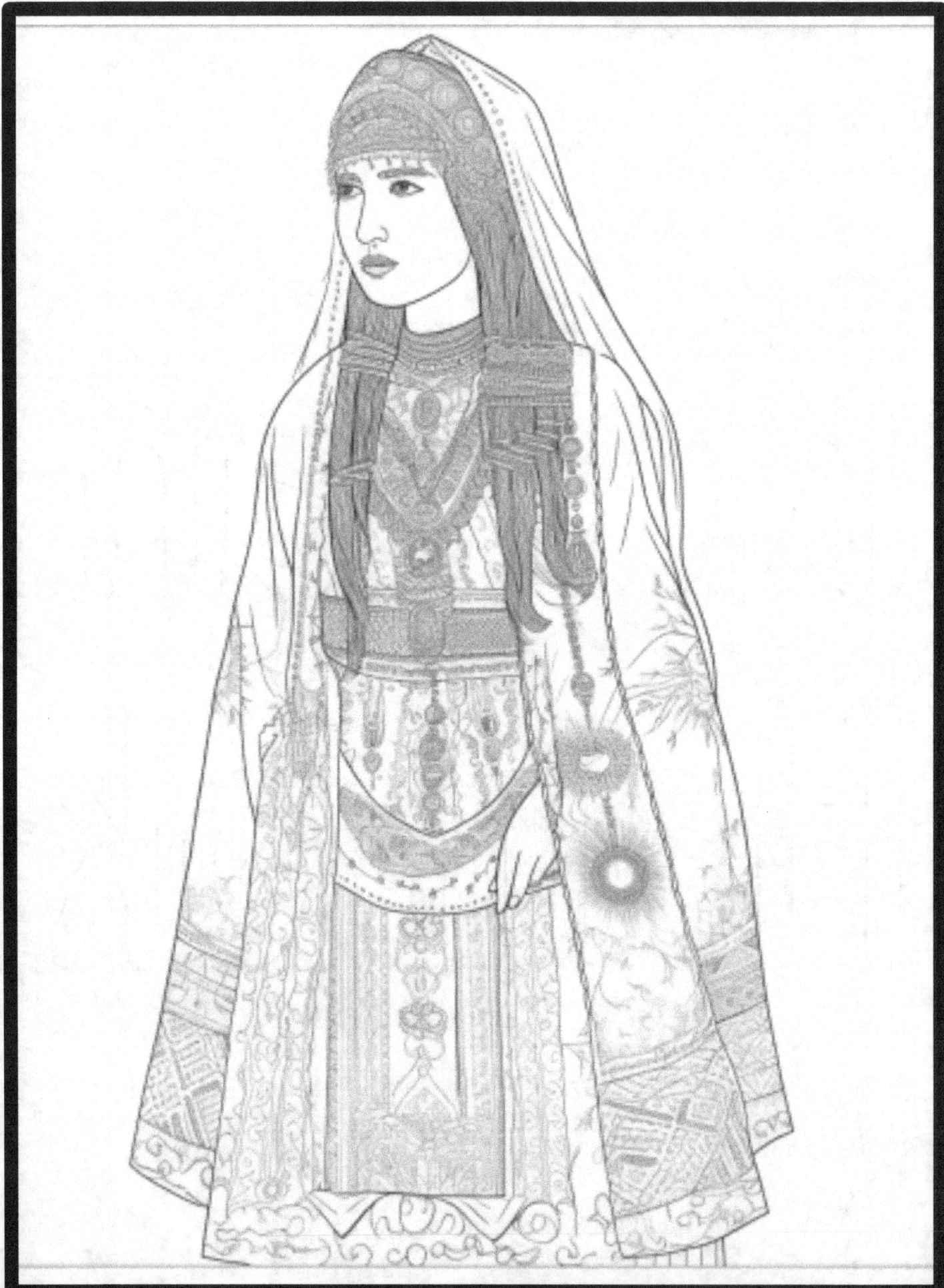

Kuchi Dress

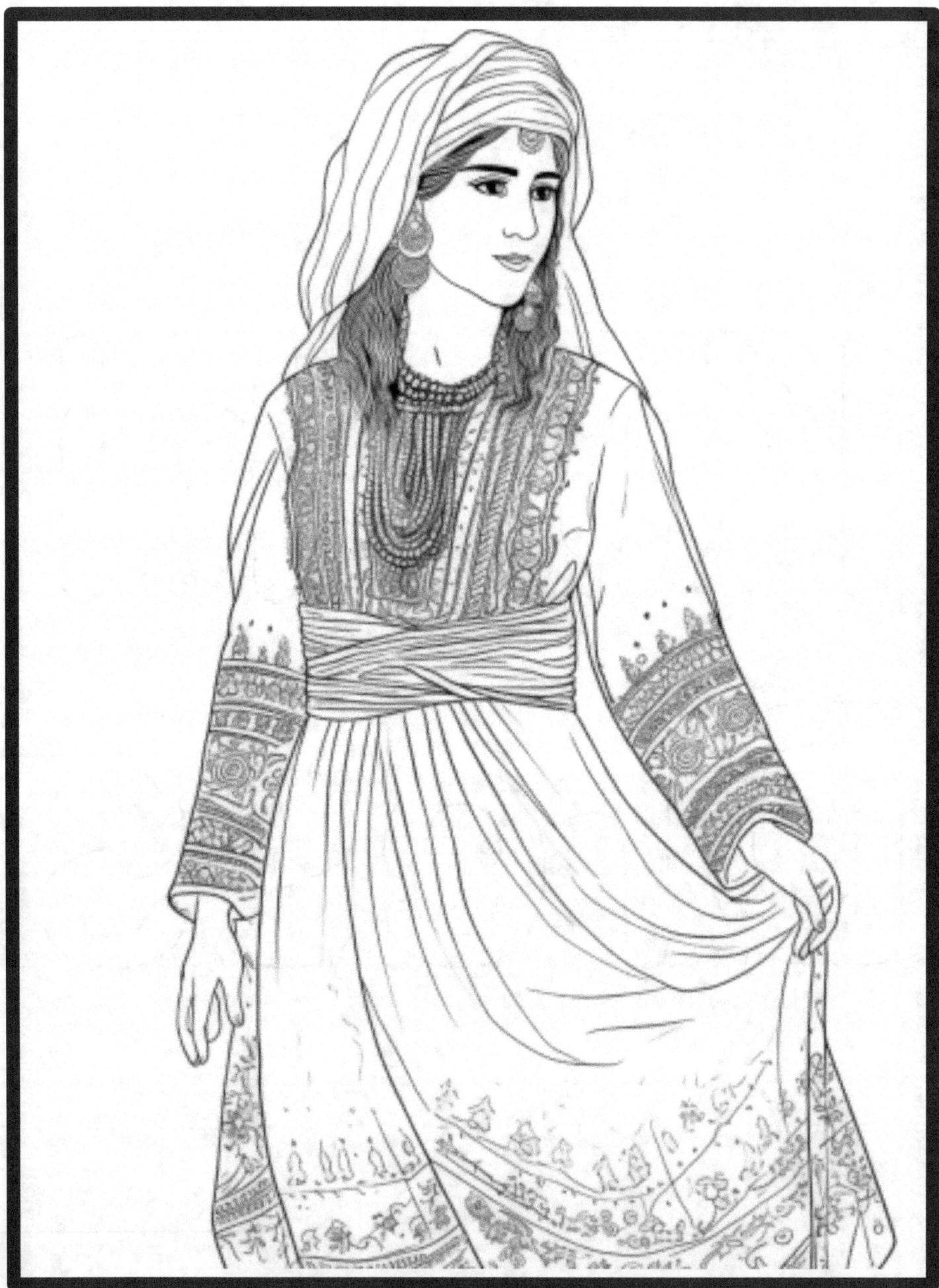

Kurdish

Dress

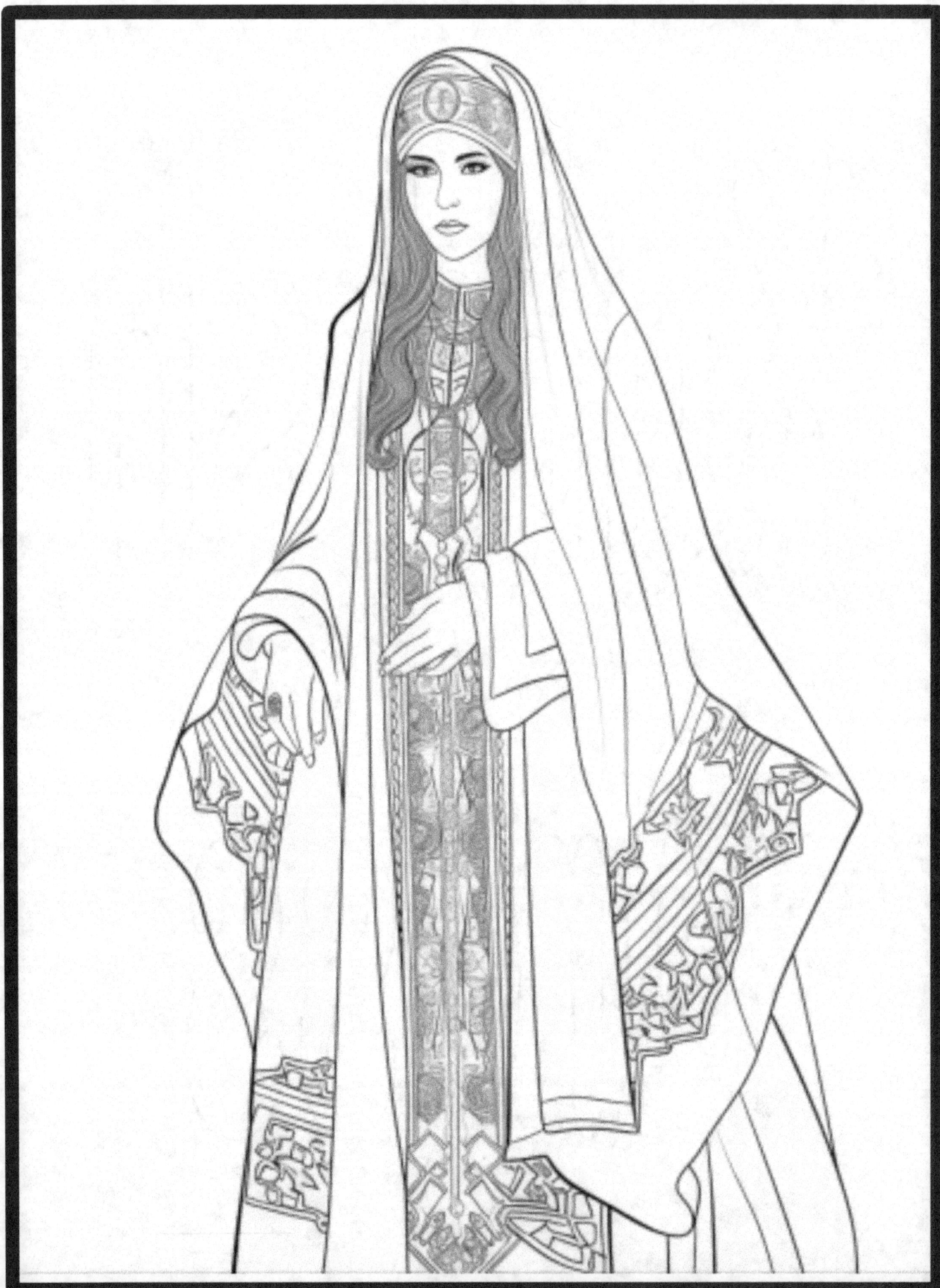

Kuwaiti Abaya

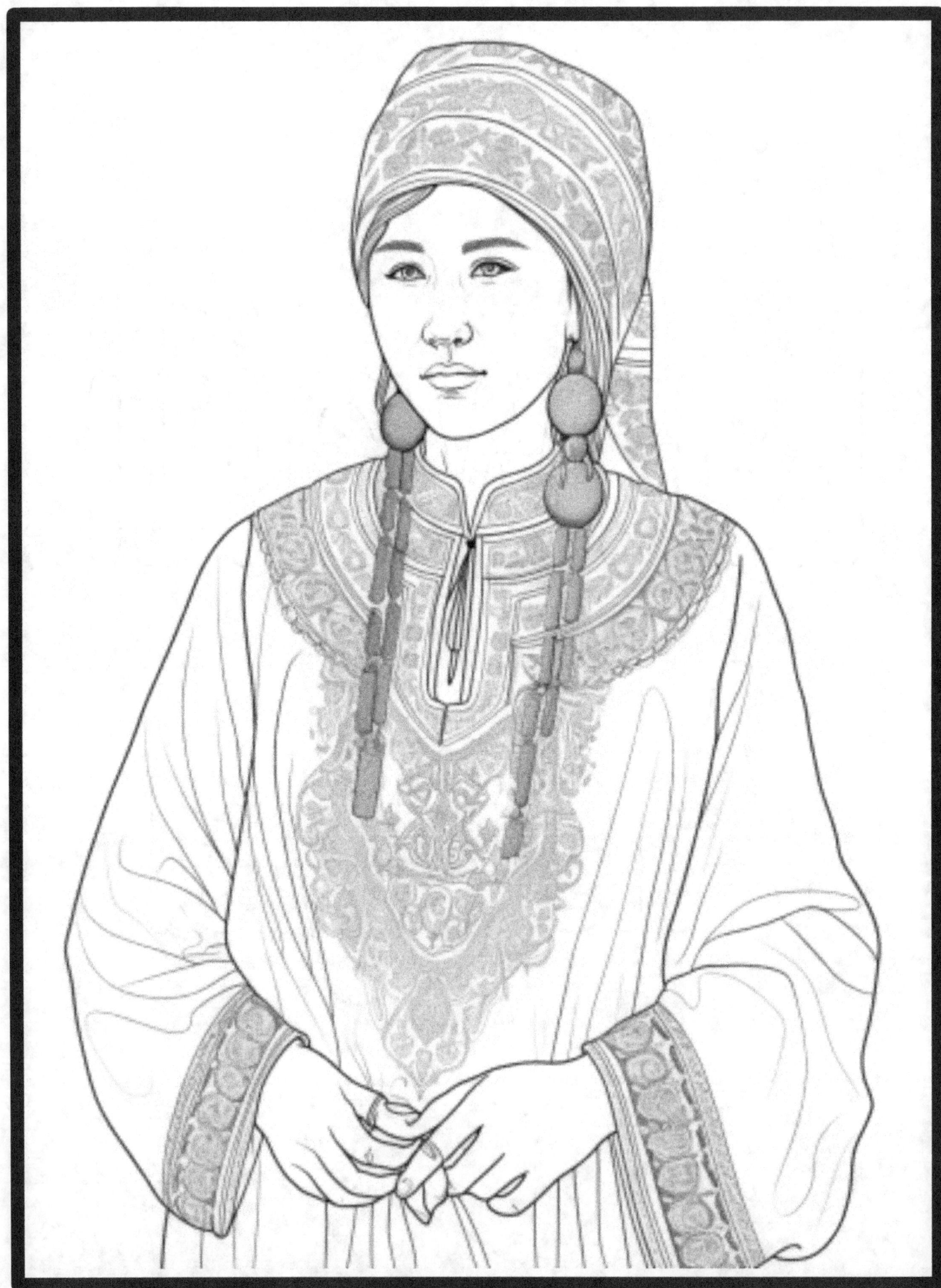

Kyrgyzstan

National Dress

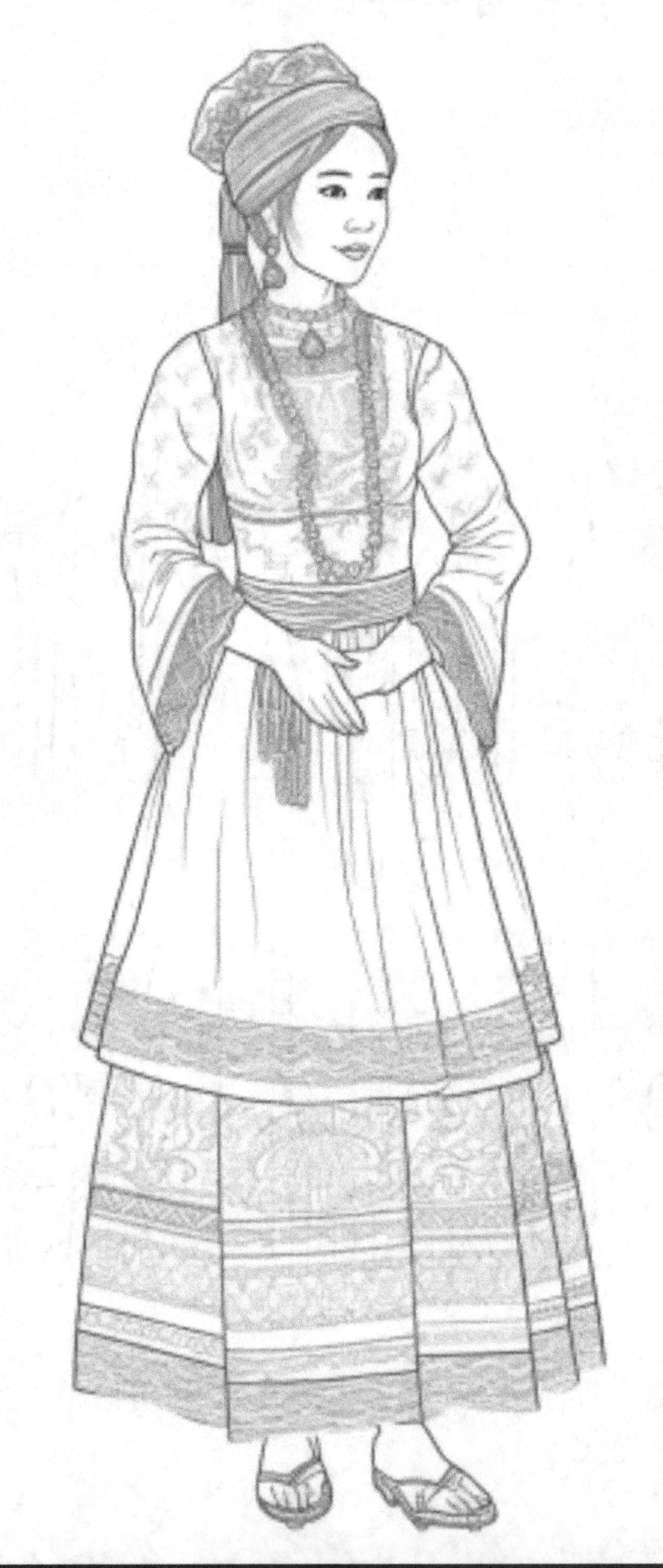

Laotion

Traditional Dress

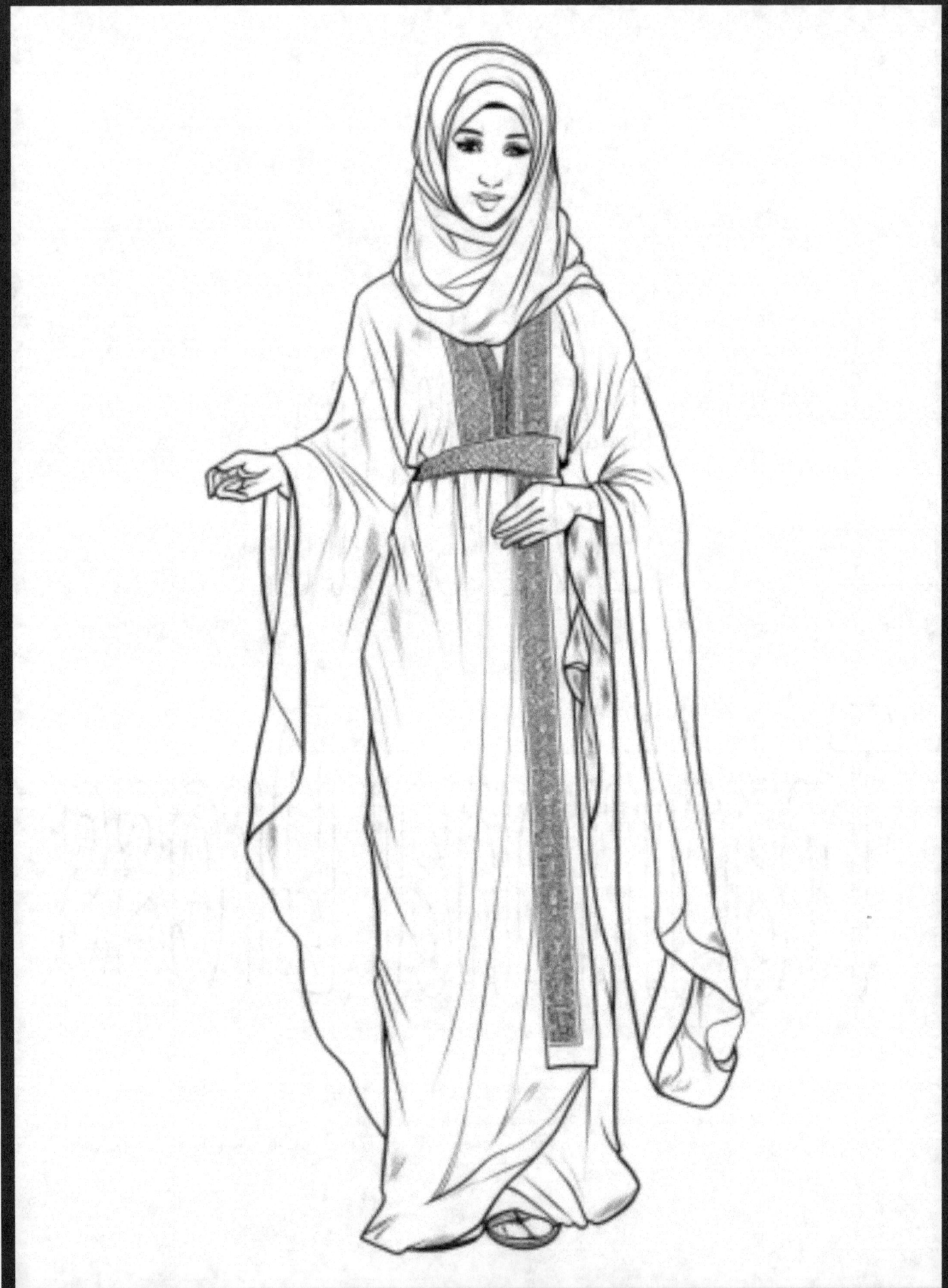

Lebanese Thobe

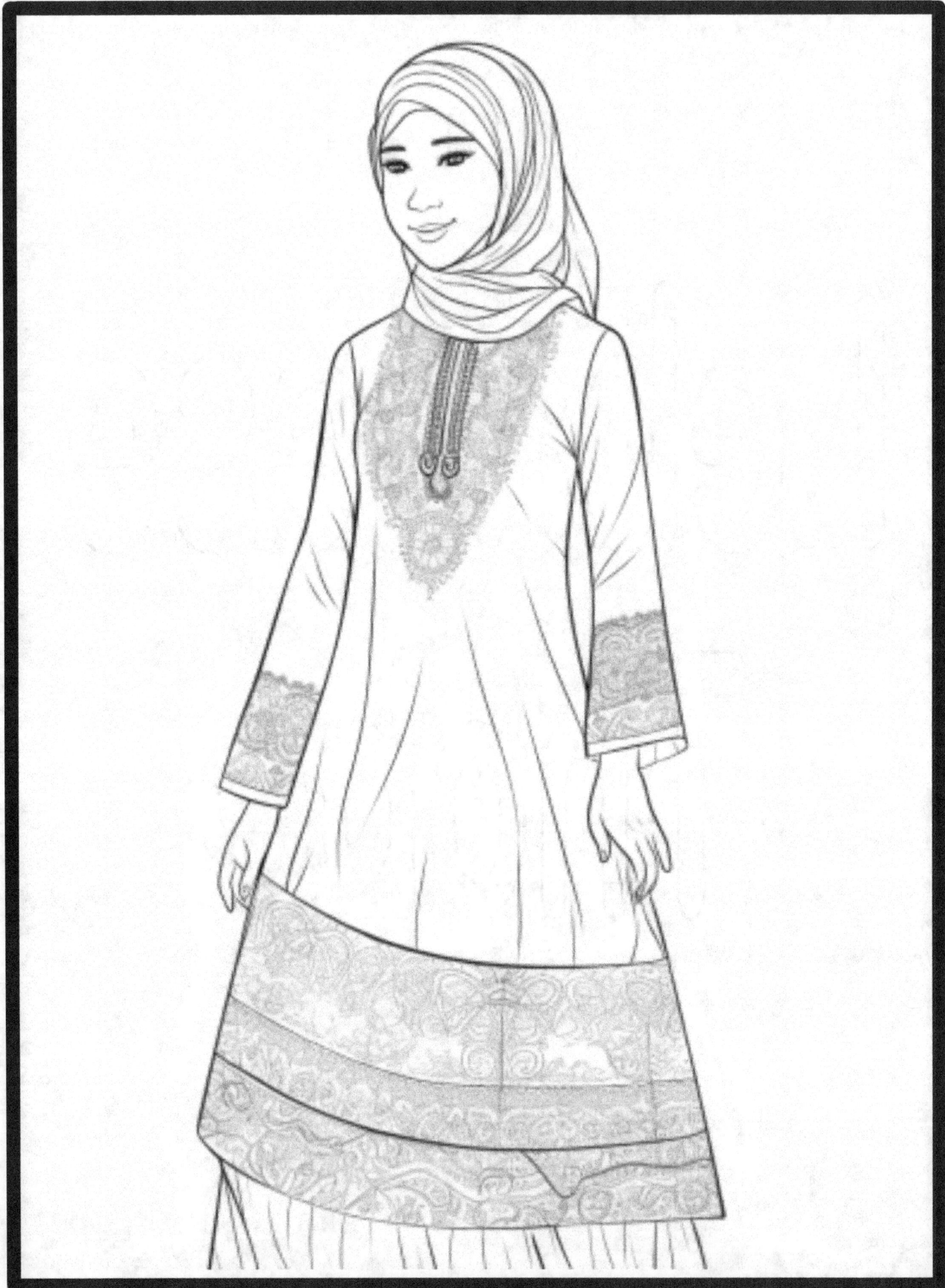

Malaysian
Baju Kurung

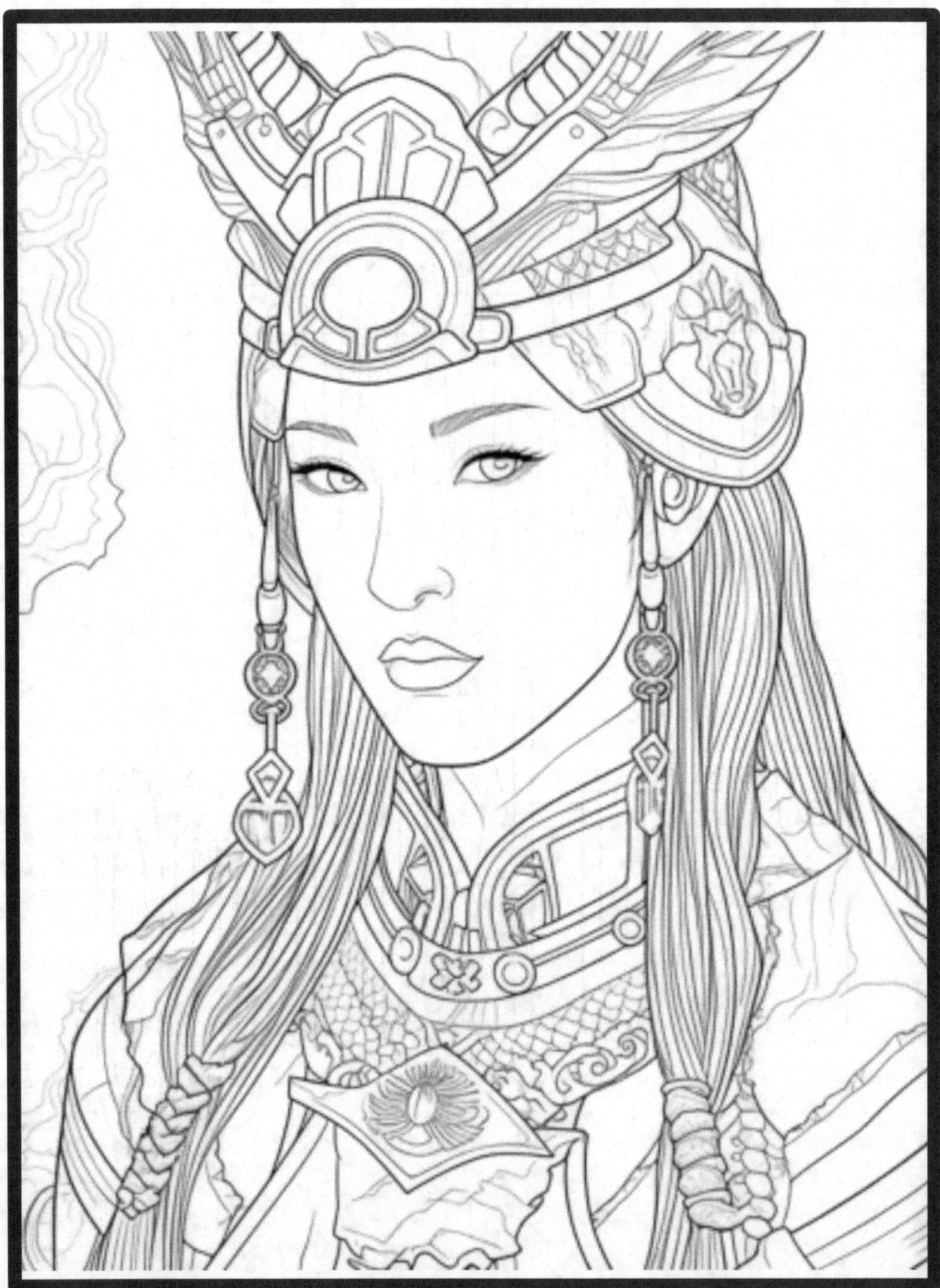

Mongolian

Deel

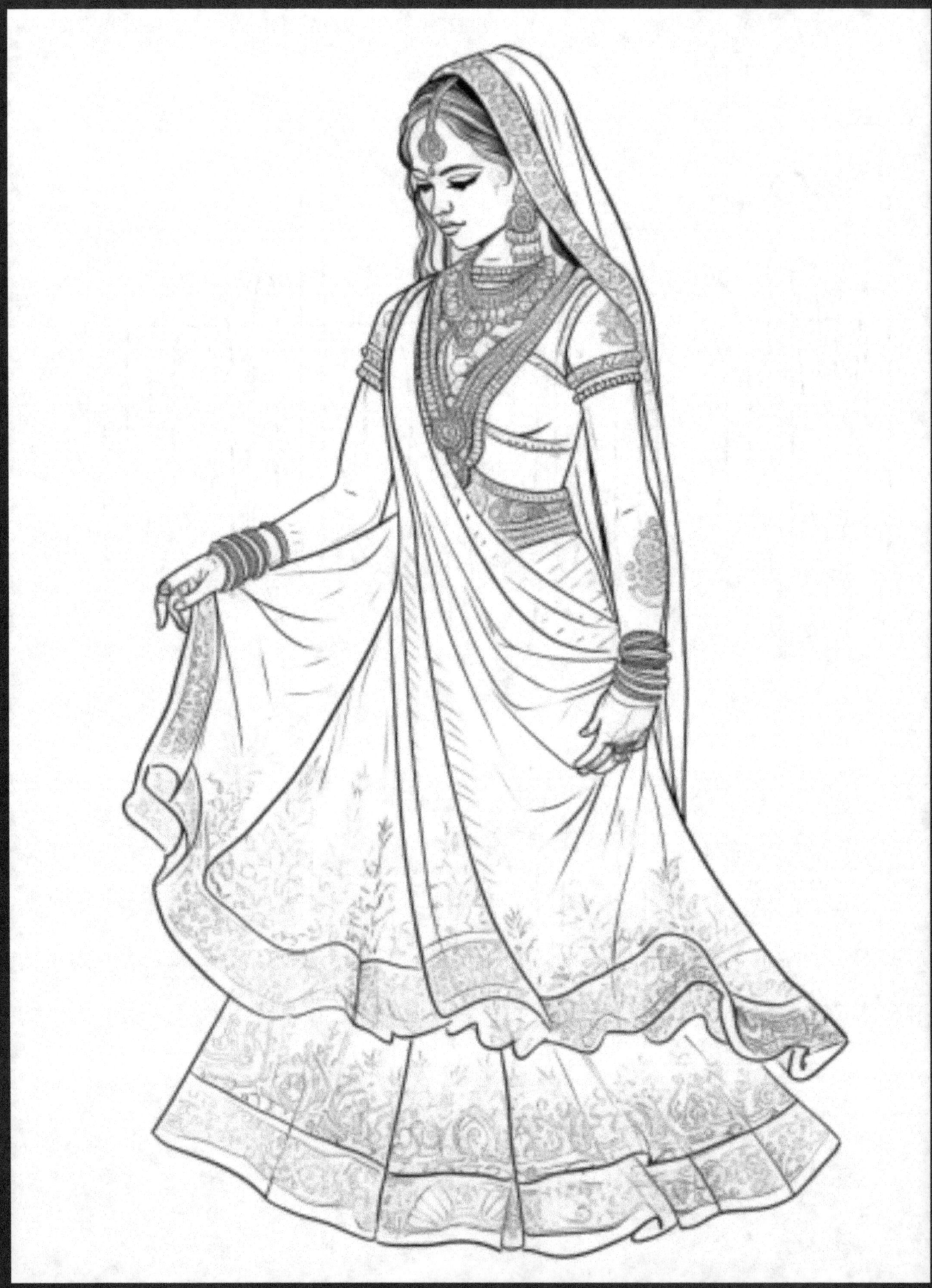

Indian Chaniya Choli

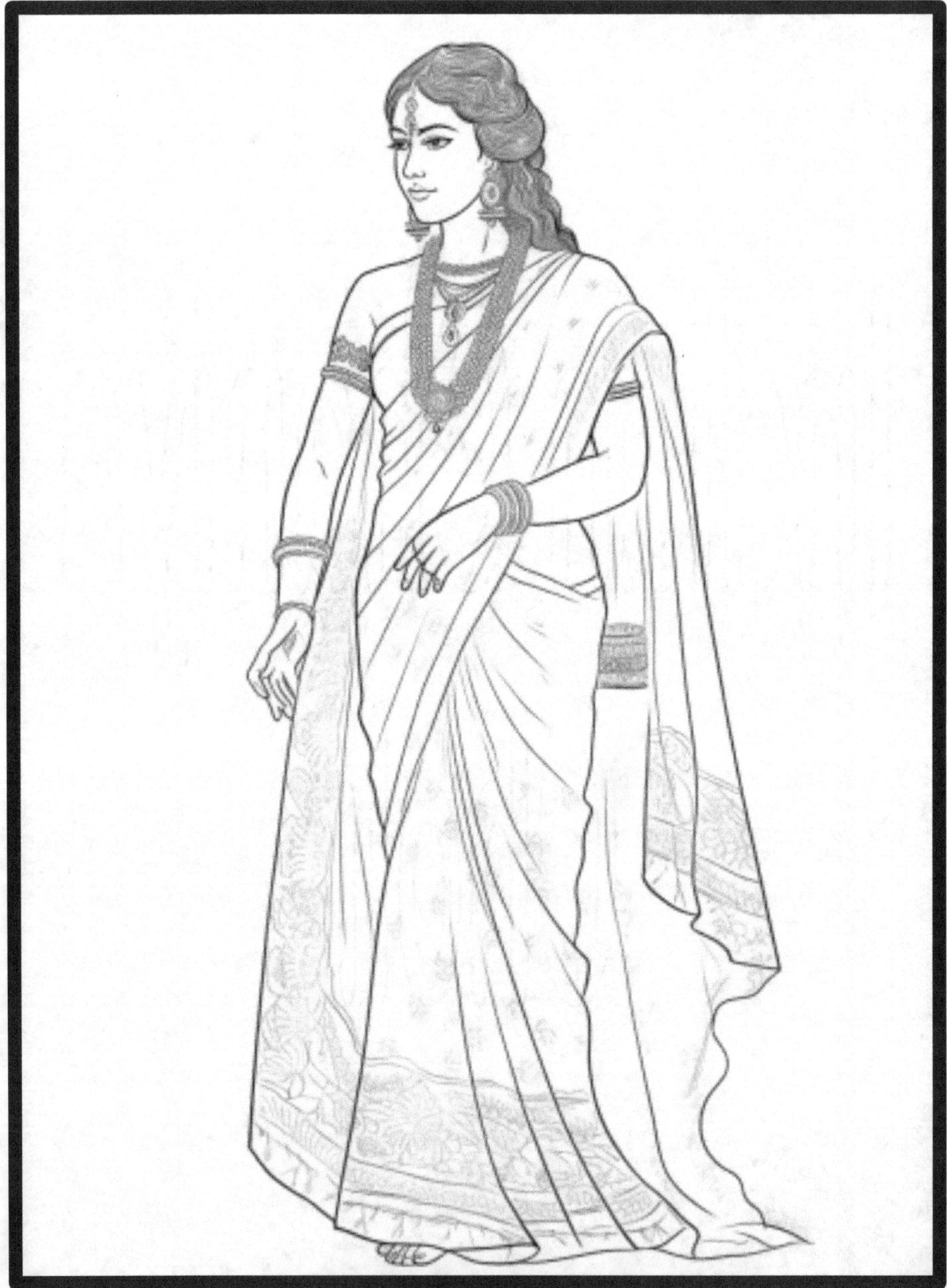

Nepalese Sari

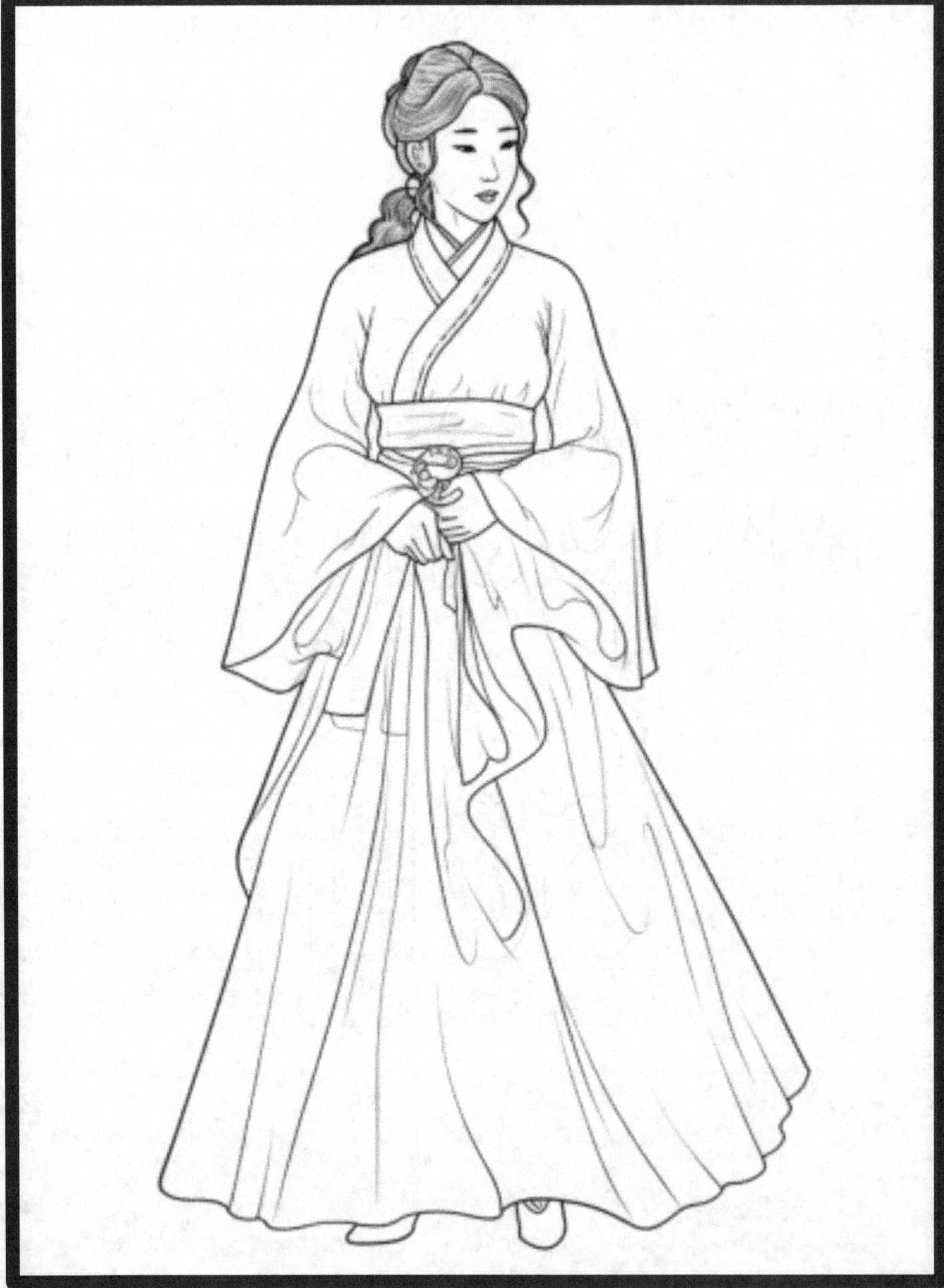

North Korean Traditional Dress

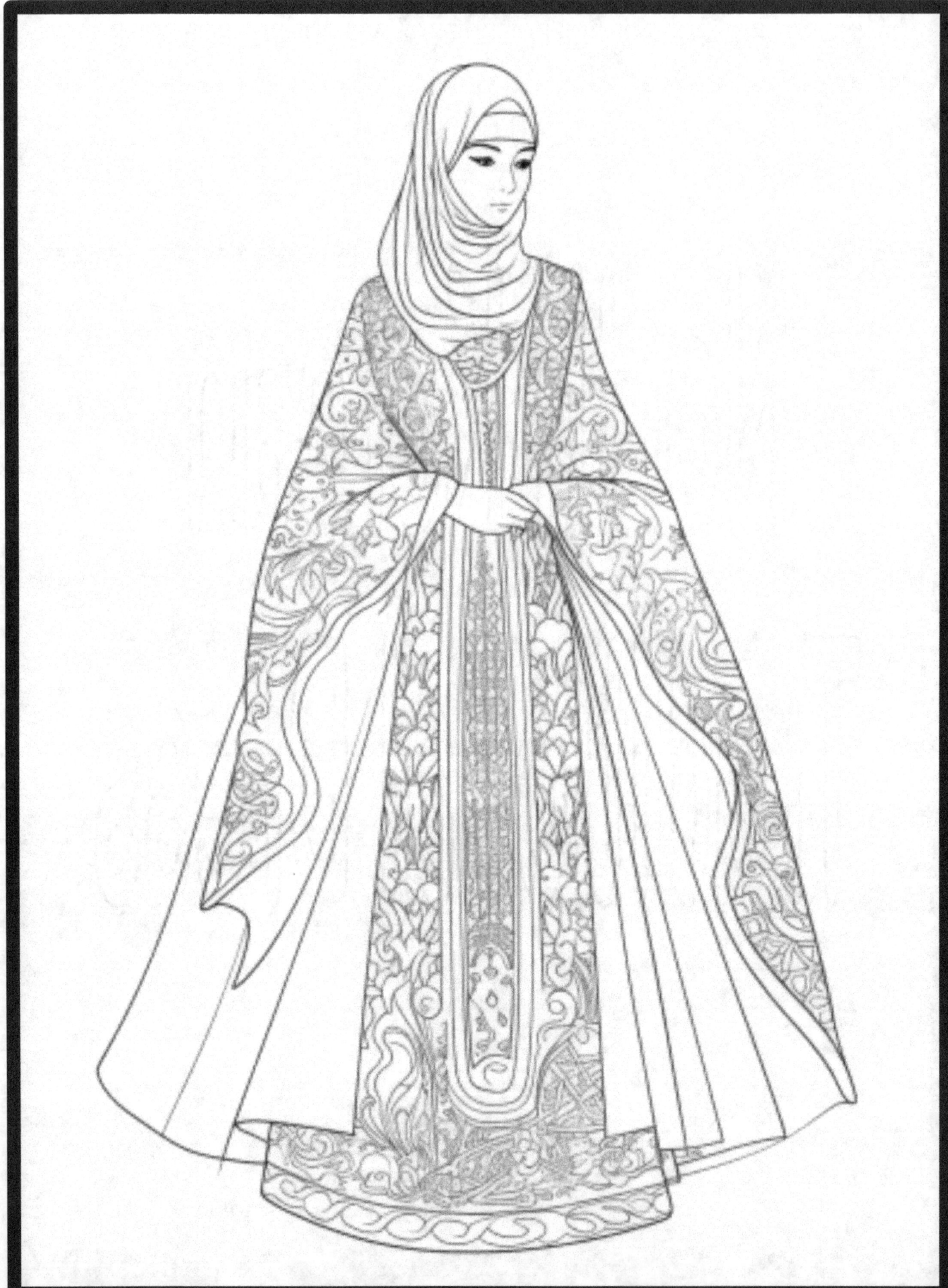

Omani

Dishdasha

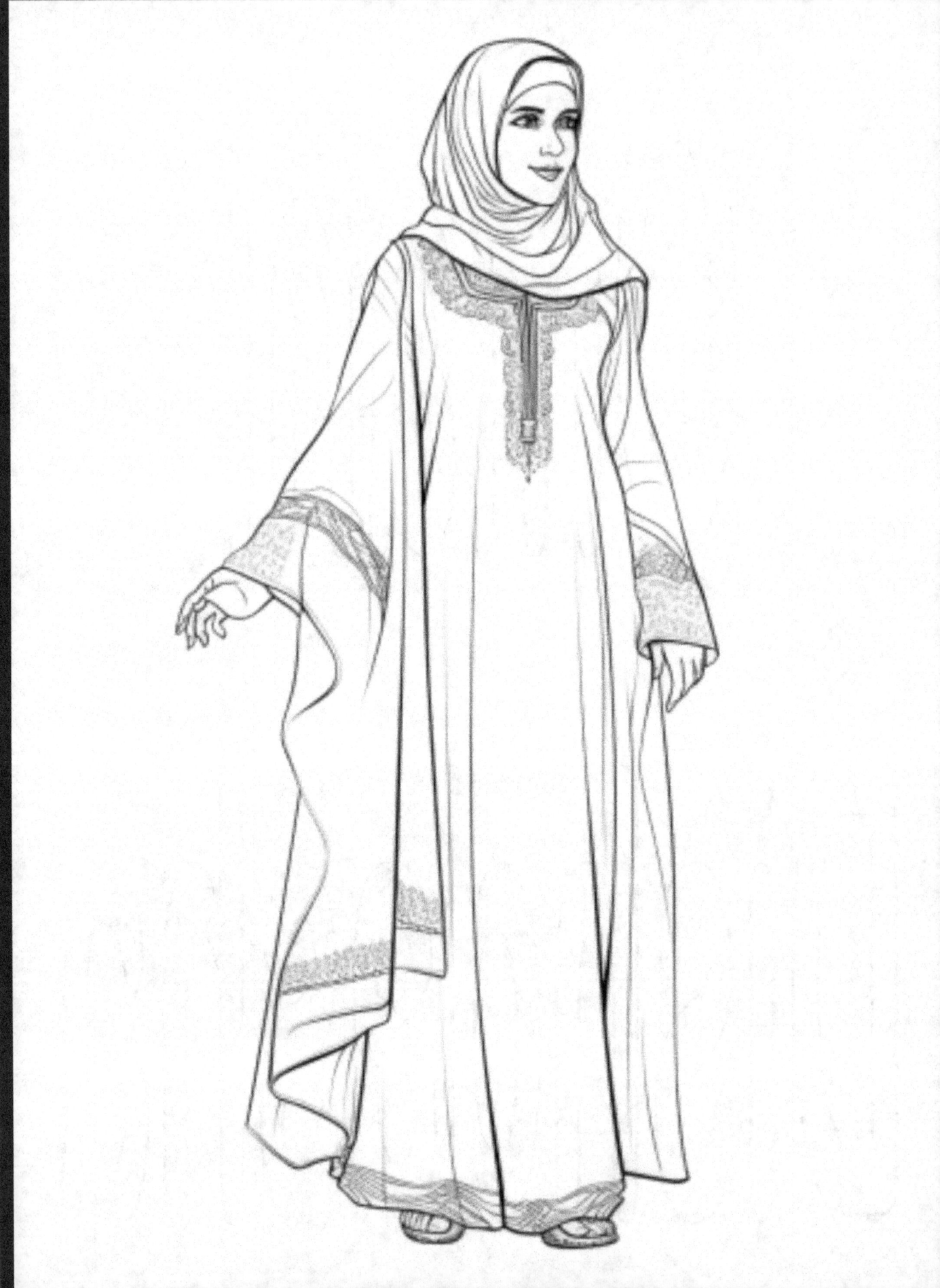

Qatari Thobe

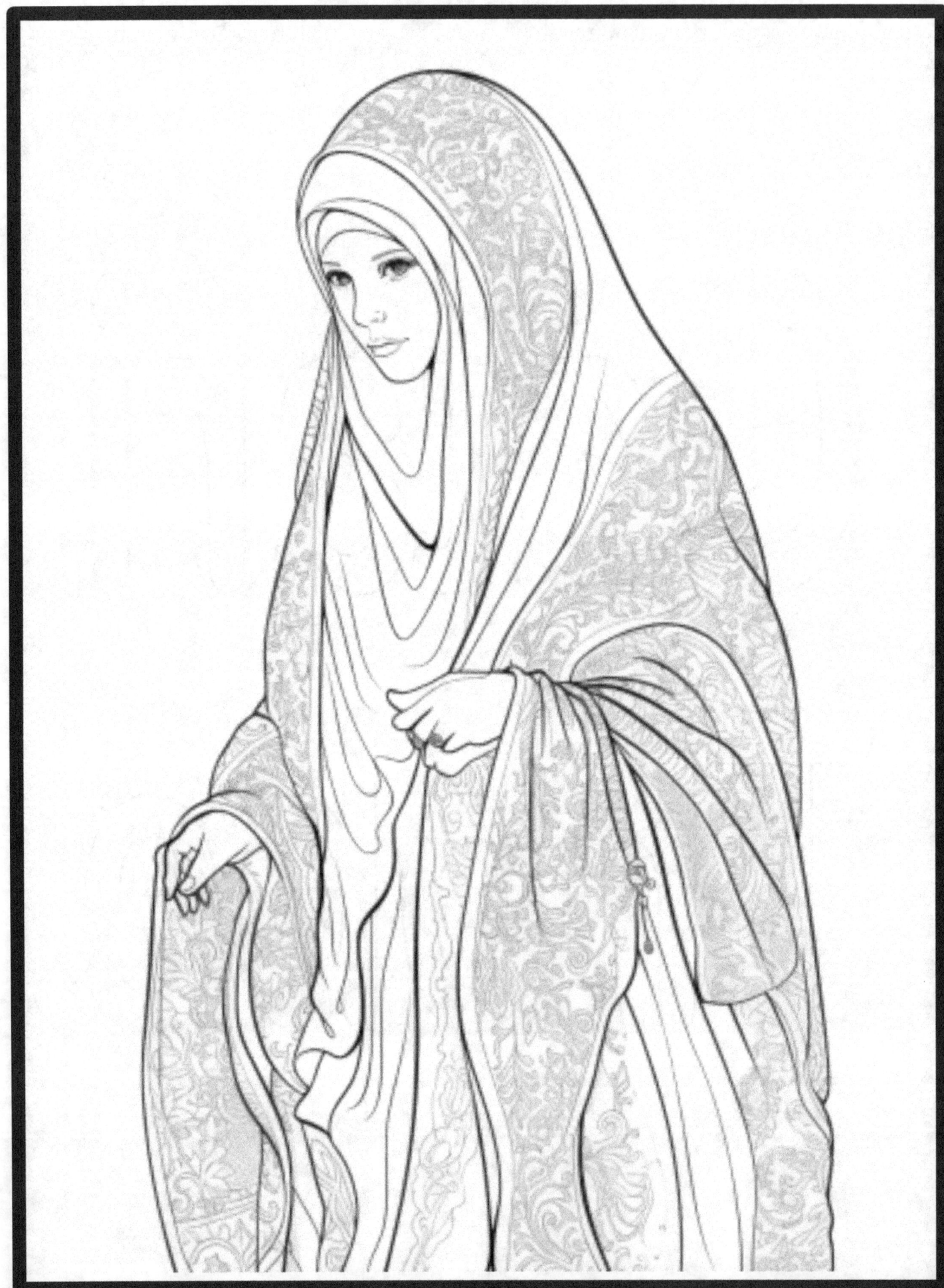

Saudi Arabian Abaya

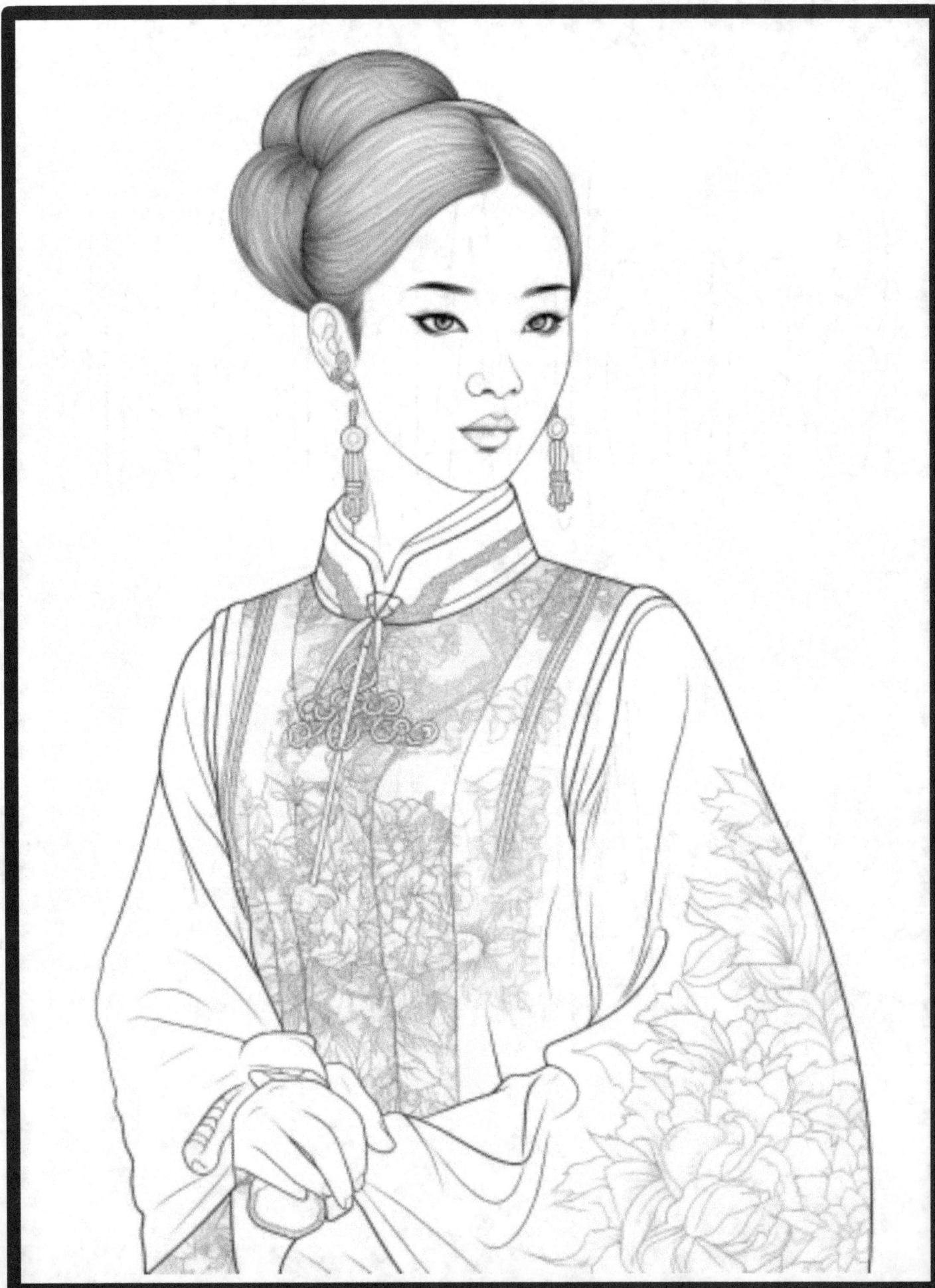

Singaporean Cheongsam

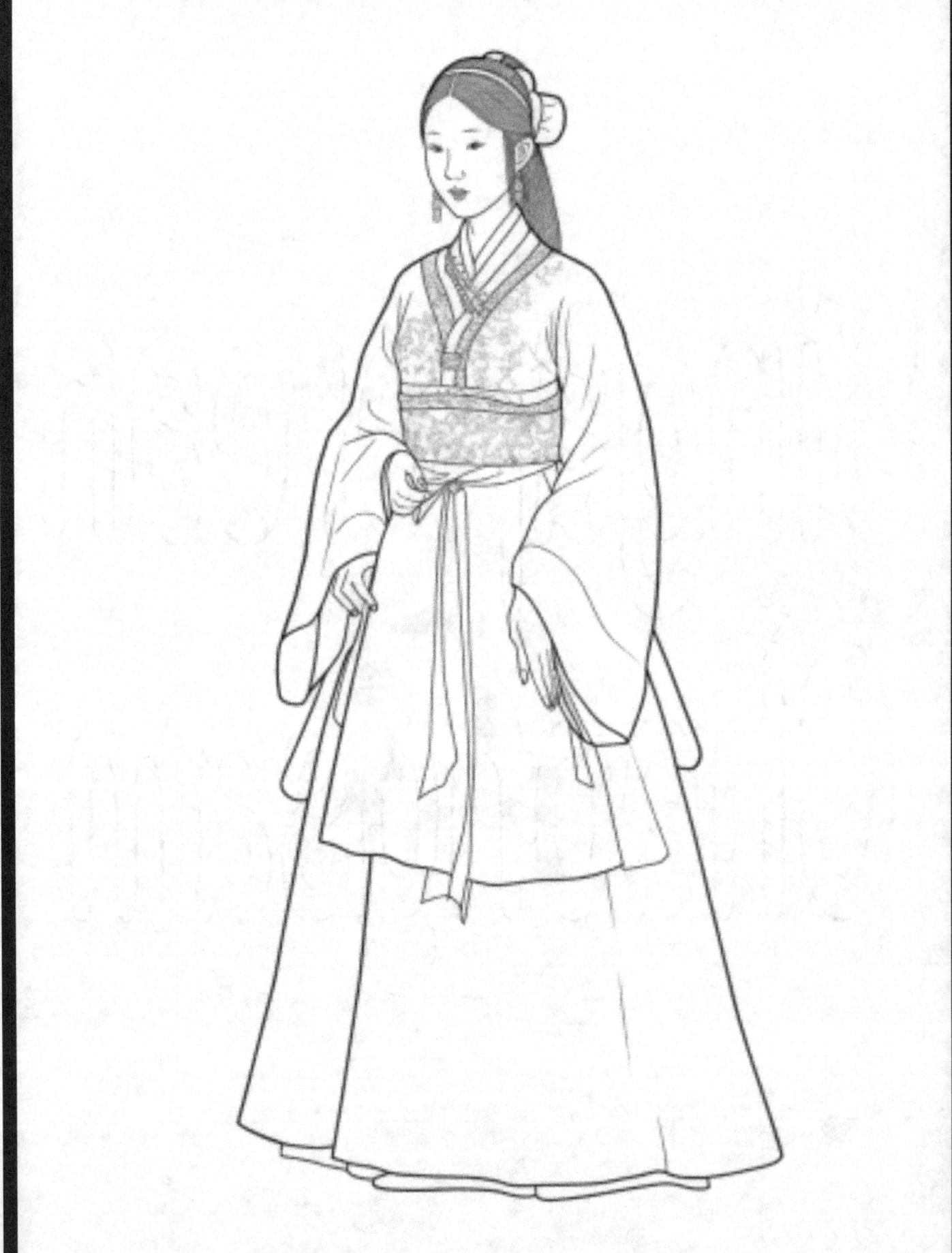

South Korean

Chima Jeogori

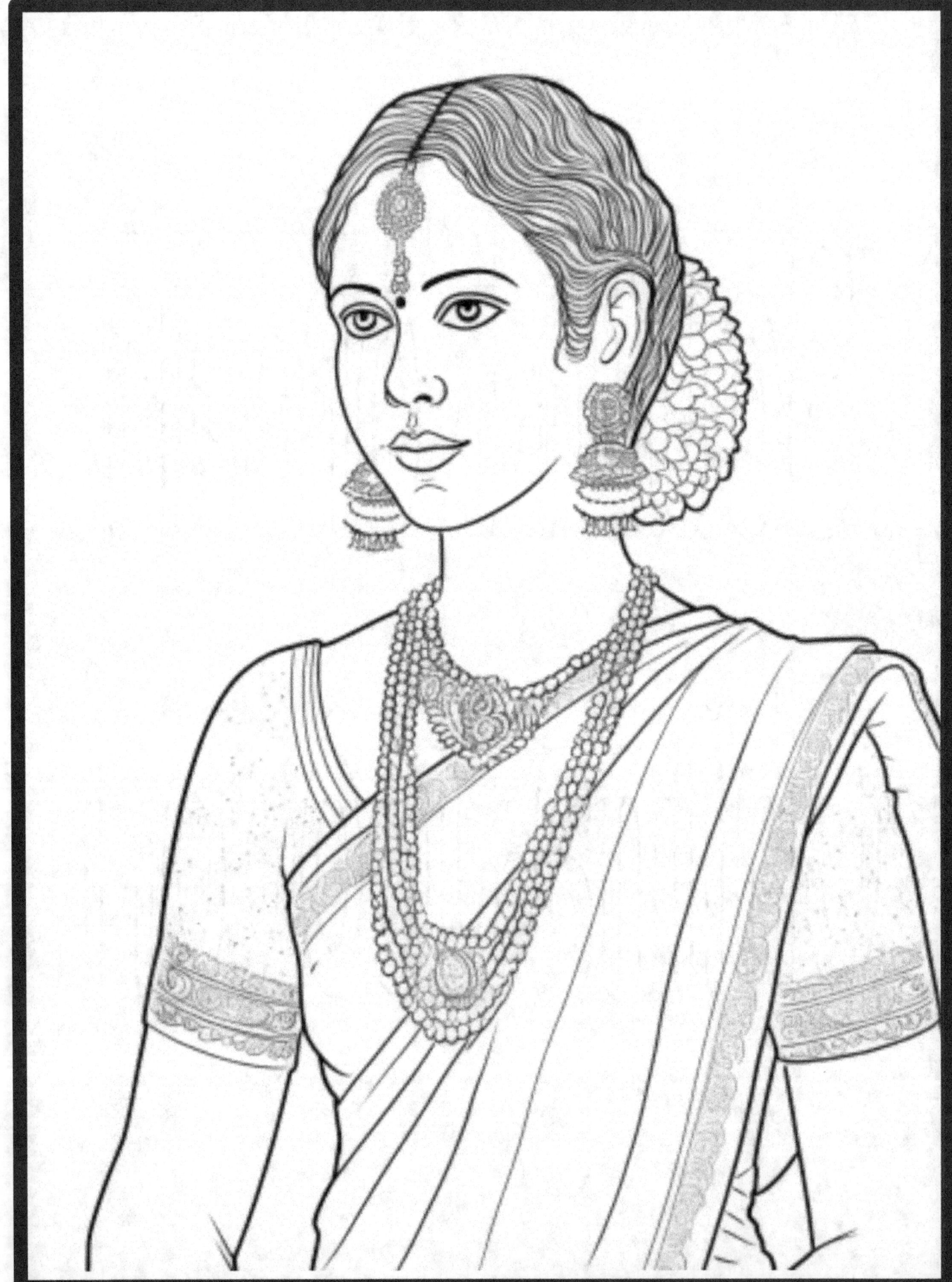

Sri Lankan Osariya

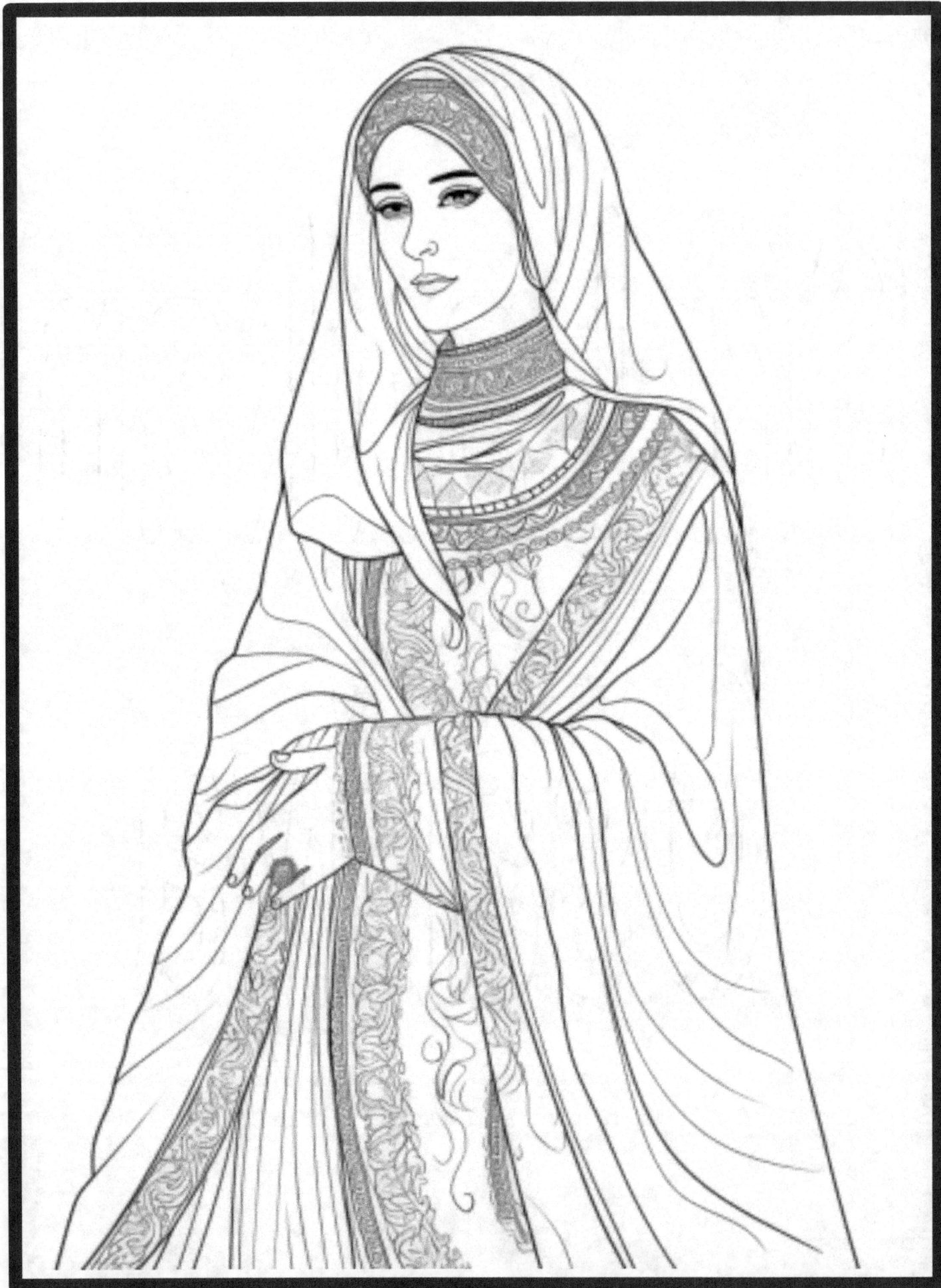

Syrian Dress

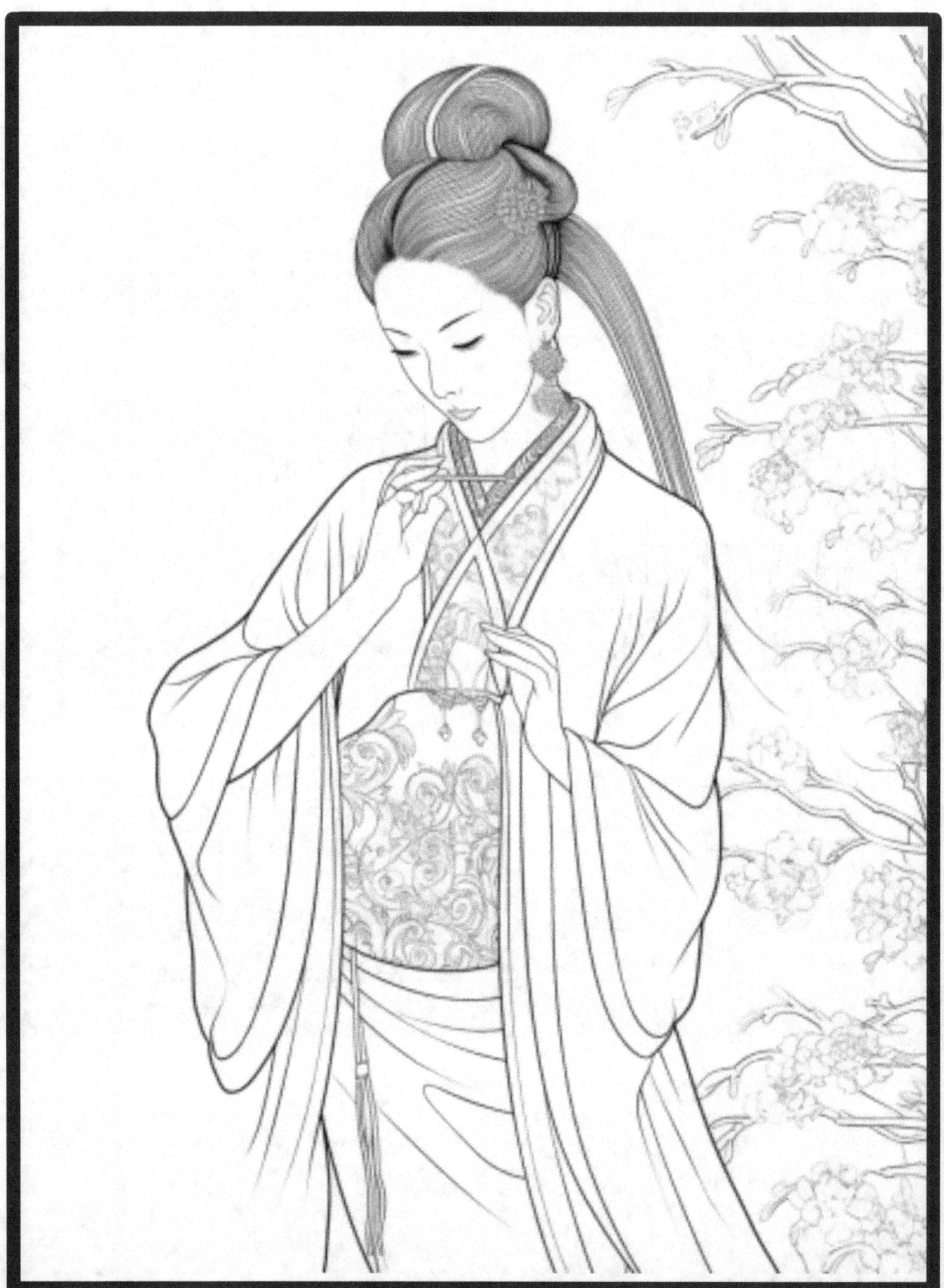

Taiwanese

Qipao

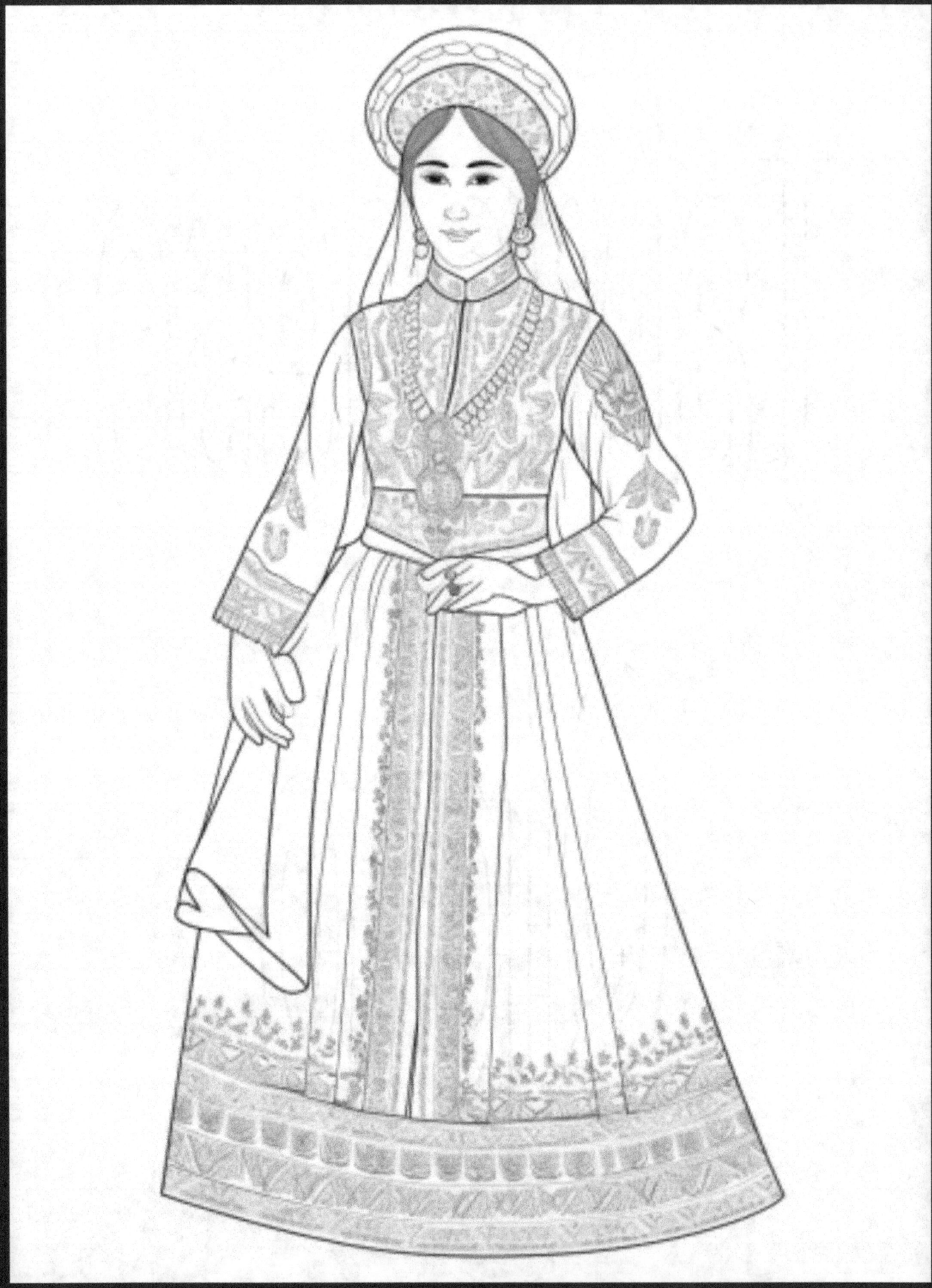

Tajikistan National Dress

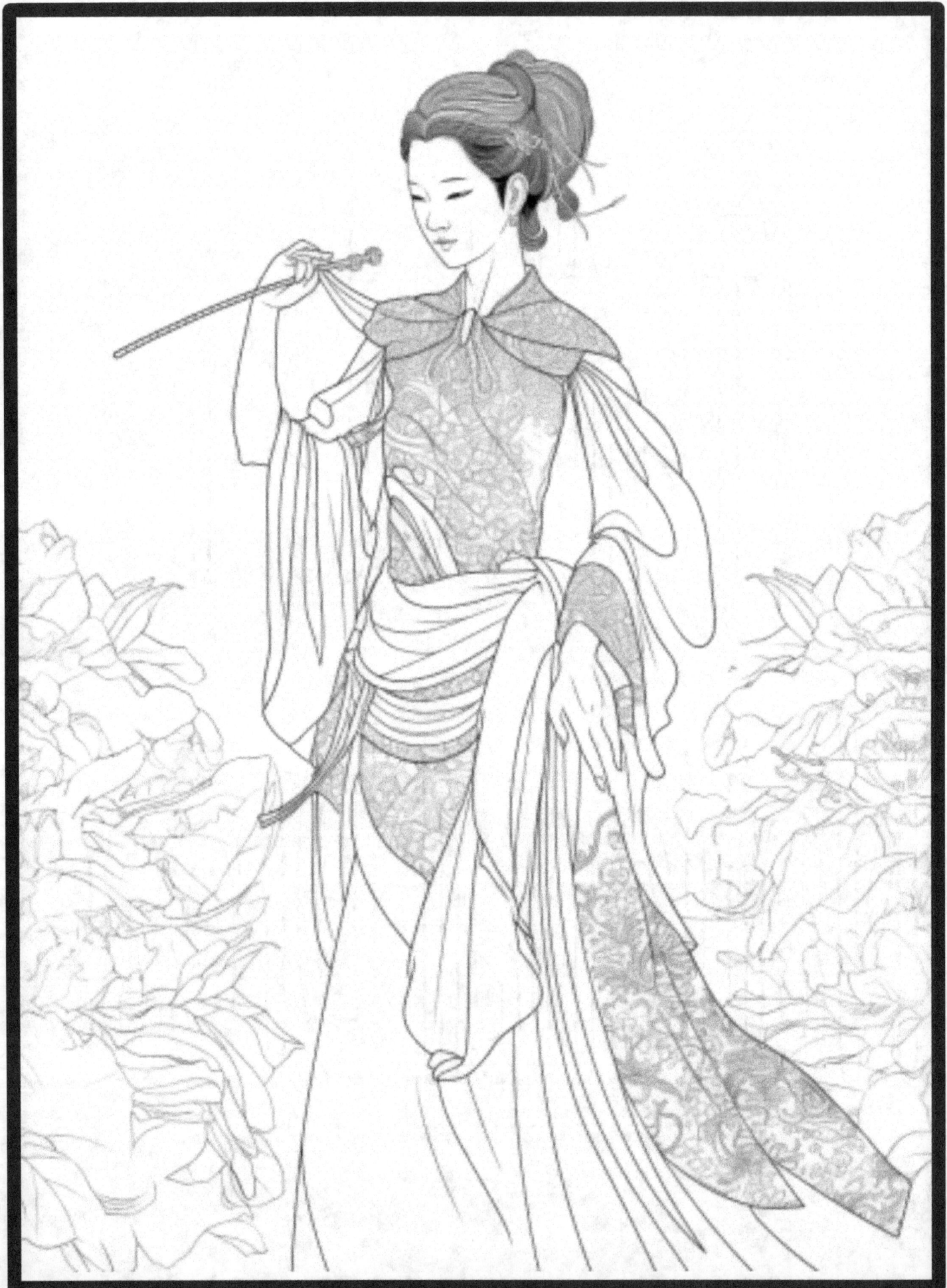

Thai Traditional Dress

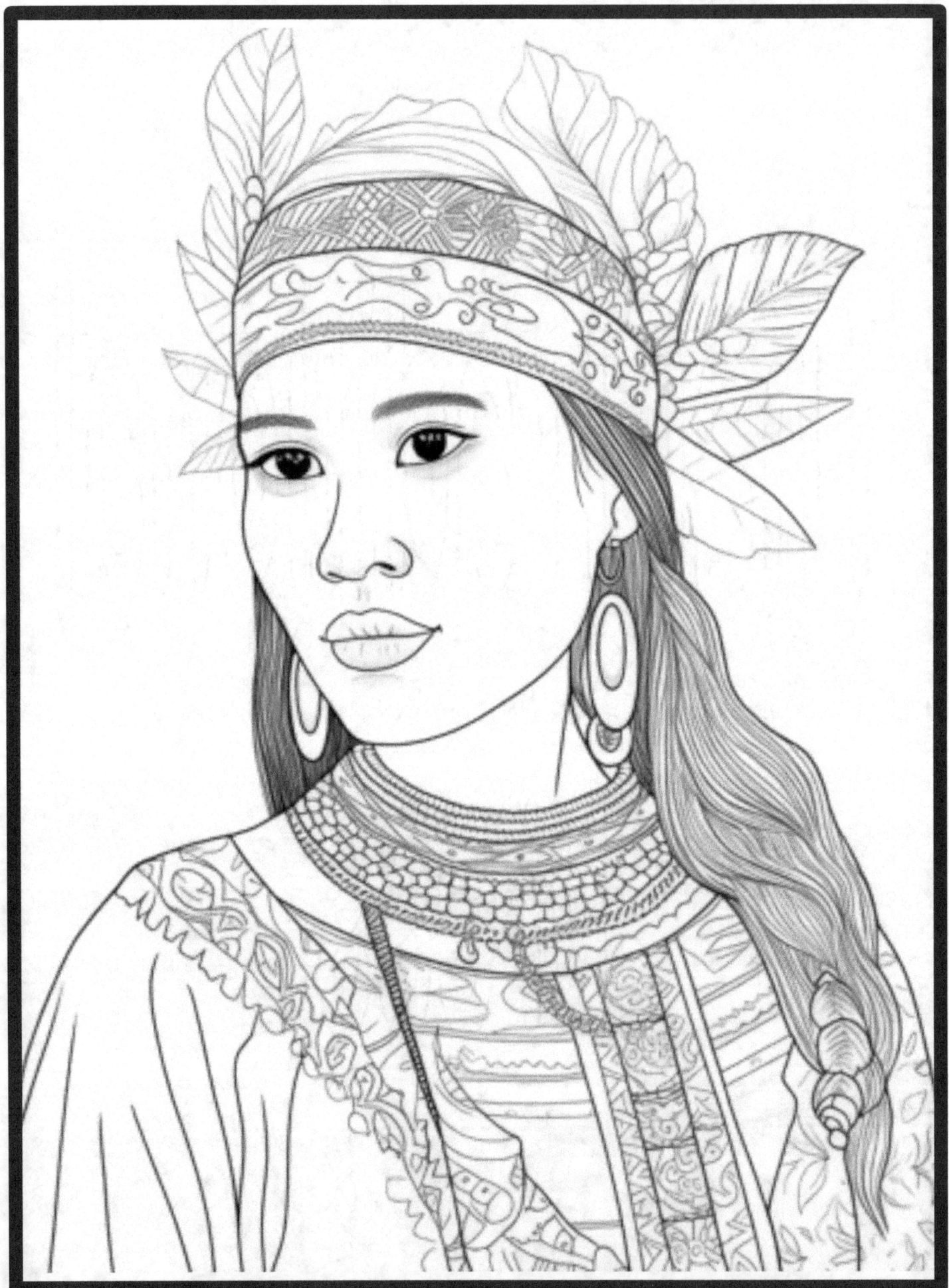

Timorese

Tais

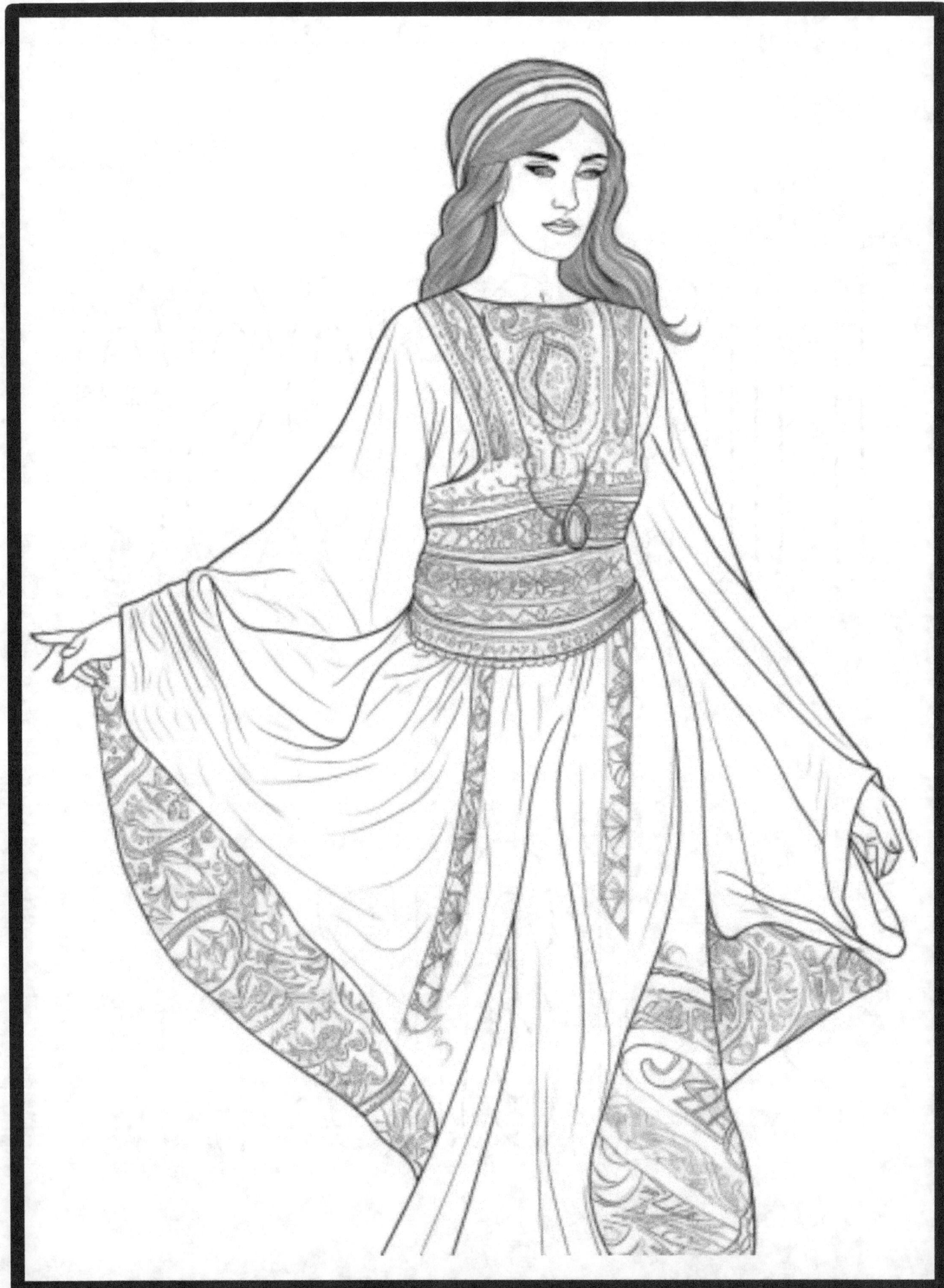

Turkish
Caftan

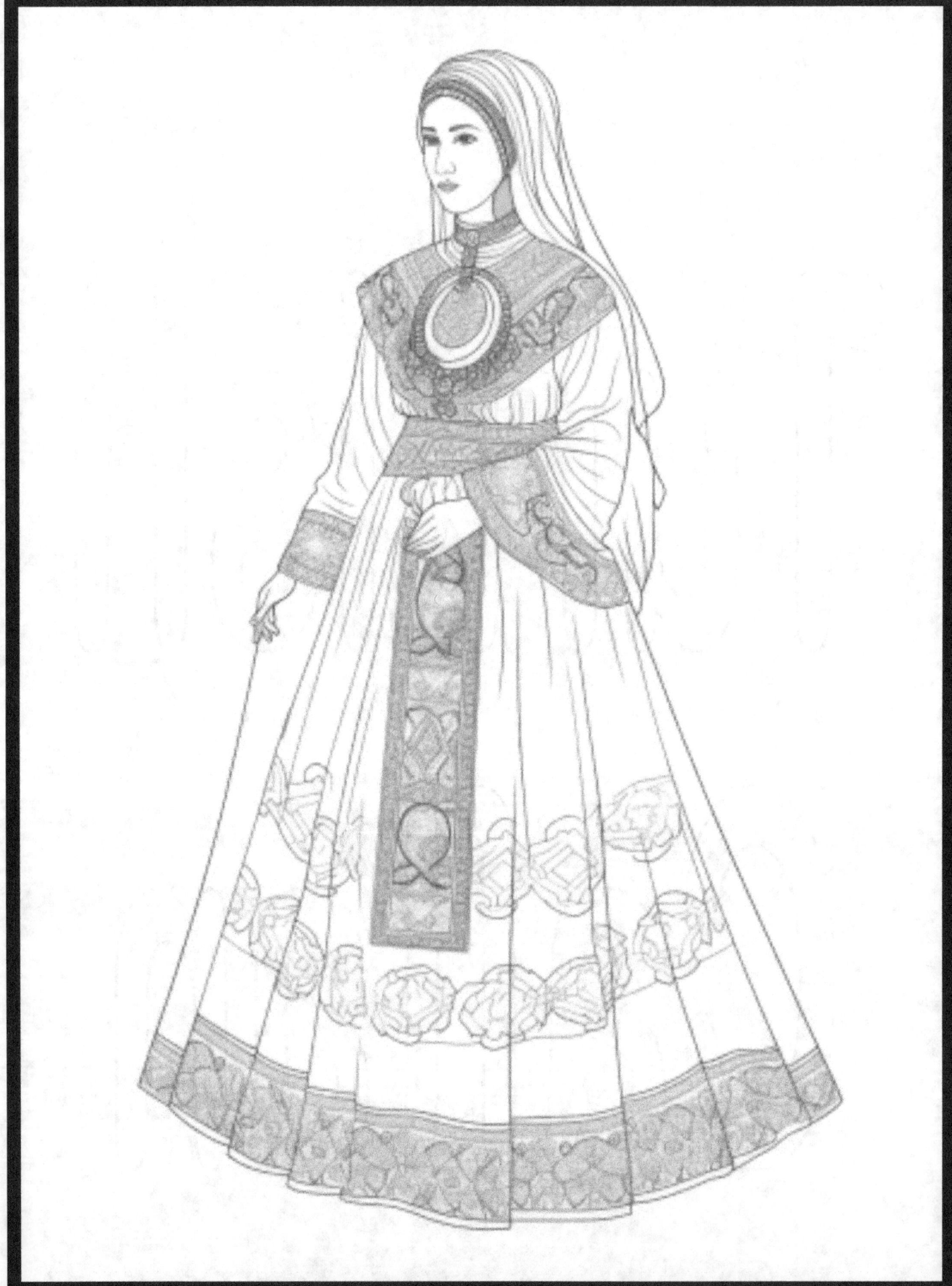

Turkmenistan

National Dress

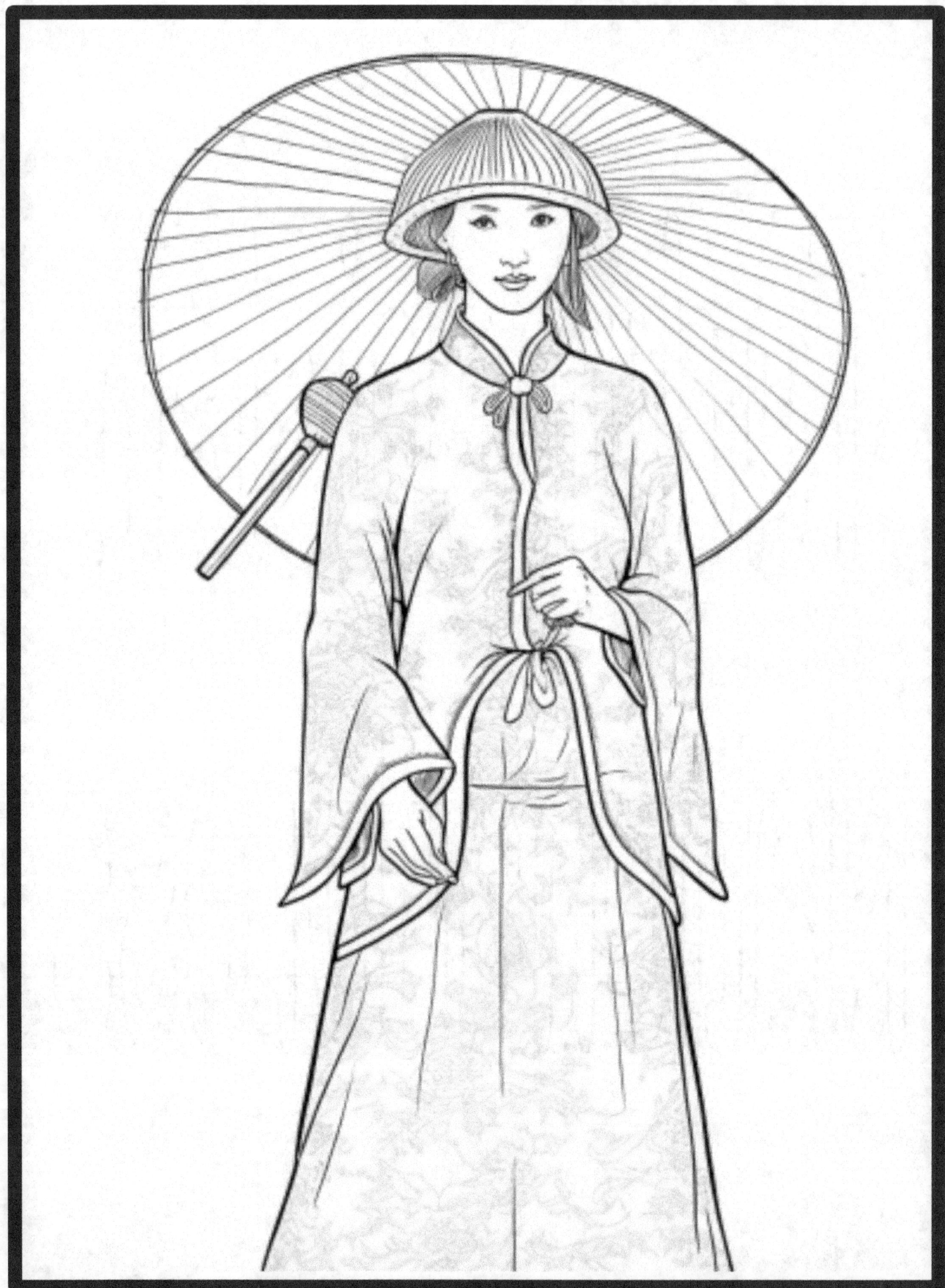

Vietnamese
Áo Dài